Byrne is the celebrated Scottish painter and writer whose
of art and rock'n'roll led to the creation of *The Slab Boys* for
Royal Court Theatre and *Tutti Frutti* and *Your Cheatin' Heart*
TV. He is currently writing a crime thriller for Faber.

D1477323

COLQUHOUN
AND
MACBRYDE

JOHN BYRNE

faber and faber

LONDON · BOSTON

First published in Great Britain in 1992
by Faber and Faber Limited
3 Queen Square London WCIN 3AU

Photoset by Parker Typesetting Service, Leicester
Printed in England by Clays Ltd, St Ives plc

All rights whatsoever in this play are strictly reserved and
application for performance etc. should be made in writing,
before rehearsals begin, to Harriet Cruikshank, Cruikshank
Casenove, 99 Old South Lambeth Road, London SW8 1XU

A CIP record for this book
is available from the British Library

ISBN 0–571–16959–7

2 4 6 8 10 9 7 5 3 1

Colquhoun and MacBryde was first performed at the Royal Court
Theatre, London, in September 1992. The cast was as follows:

COLQUHOUN	David O'Hara
MACBRYDE	Ken Stott
JANKEL ADLER/MURIEL	Christopher Ettridge
GEORGE BARKER/ARP WARDEN	Julian Firth
DYLAN THOMAS/JOURNALIST	Giles Thomas
CORPORAL/WAITER/BAILIFF/ PHOTOGRAPHER	Morgan Jones

Director	Lindsay Posner
Designer	John Byrne
Lighting	Gerry Jenkinson
Sound	Bryan Bowen

ACT ONE

A sofa and an easel. At the easel, ROBERT COLQUHOUN, *dark, lugubrious. On the sofa, face-down, naked,* ROBERT MACBRYDE. COLQUHOUN *steps back from life painting, squints at it.*

COLQUHOUN: Rest.

> (*A faint snore from the sofa.*)
> Rest!

MACBRYDE: Waaah!

COLQUHOUN: Nineteen thirty-seven . . . the year Hitler bombs Guernica, the Romantic period is reclaimed and comprehensively restructured by critics and artists, *Lilliput* is published under Stefan Lorent's editorship, and Mrs MacFarlane has her gas meter broken into and her ovaries removed . . . what else? Oh, yes . . . the *Kilmarnock Advertiser*, in a 'Stop Press' paragraph, reports that the 'Two Roberts' . . . Colquhoun and MacBryde, have graduated with *distinction* from Glasgow School of Art . . .

MACBRYDE: Ma bum's itchy.

COLQUHOUN: . . . Bobby MacBryde . . . a year older than me, a foot shorter . . . first block I bumped into comin' up the front steps of Mackintosh's Art Nouveau 'extravaganza' . . . I was in my school blazer from night school, he was sporting a pair of hand-painted tartan jodhpurs . . . lent me a stick of charcoal and paid us both into the pictures later that same night . . . *Les Enfants du Paradis* at the recently opened Cosmo in Rose Street, I thought I was going to die, I was that happy . . . ugly bastard, isn't he?

MACBRYDE: Not only is ma bum itchy, I'm also extremely vexed, Robert.

COLQUHOUN: Mrs MacFarlane's our current landlady, just in case you're wondering . . . what're you 'extremely vexed' about now, Bobby son? He's always 'vexed' about somethin' or other. Eh?

MACBRYDE: We havenae found ourselves yet.

COLQUHOUN: Try not to clench your buttocks like that, it's dead annoyin'.

(*He resumes life painting.*)

MACBRYDE: I mean, you don't get guys comin' outta medical school after however many years an' goin' 'What now?', do you?

COLQUHOUN: Not unless they went there to study motor mechanics in the first place, no. Stop swivellin' your head round, will you?

MACBRYDE: Aye, an' stop you actin' obtuse, you know fine well what I'm gettin' at, you should be able to pick out a 'Colquhoun' or a 'MacBryde' a mile off by now, same way you can pick out a Picasso or a Pinturicchio, right?

COLQUHOUN: Now you are jokin'. I defy anybody, Berenson included, to pick out a Pinturicchio from *this* close without a big label with 'Pinturicchio' printed on it in letters this size . . . what's all this sudden soul-searching in aid of anyhow? We're hardly five weeks out the Art School, we've got the next forty years to 'find' ourselves.

MACBRYDE: By which time we'll not be able to catch up . . . for Christ's sake, Rab, look at what's happenin' in Paris . . . London . . . New York . . .

COLQUHOUN: What?

MACBRYDE: . . . absolutely bugger all, that's what I'm sayin'. What's required is for a coupla 'Young Turks' to grab the Art World by the scruff of the neck an' shake it till its teeth rattle . . .

COLQUHOUN: What were you just told about clenchin' your buttocks?

MACBRYDE: . . . I am not clenchin' ma flamin' . . . ohyah!

COLQUHOUN: Aw, for God's sake . . .

(*Chucks brushes down.* MACBRYDE *reaches underneath his belly and produces small, over-ripe banana.*)
. . . what's that?

MACBRYDE: You never clapped eyes on a banana before? My, we have led a sheltered life, Robert . . . Here, d'you want a sook?

COLQUHOUN: No, I do not want a sook, I want to know how you came by the wherewithal to furnish yourself with a banana?

Have you been dippin' into them gas meter takings? That dough was for buyin' decent watercolour paper, not for you to squander on exotica, I'm fed up paintin' on old sugar pokes and toilet rolls, get back into your pose, dammit!

MACBRYDE: I havenae relinquished ma bloody pose, chuck shoutin' at . . .

(*Breaks off.*) . . . hold on, since when did we ever have toilet rolls in these digs? All I can recall is the *Reynolds News* cut up into wee jaggy squares an' specially selected non-absorbent pages from the *News of the World* . . .

COLQUHOUN: Which is precisely where you're goin' to wind up if you don't stop annoyin' me . . . 'Male Nude With Small Banana and Big Ideas Stabbed In The Gorbals By Unknown Assailant' . . .

MACBRYDE: Correction, Rab . . . '*Completely* Unknown Assailant'.

COLQUHOUN: That's right, rub it in . . . how the hell am I supposed to start making a name for myself when you'll not let me finish this?

MACBRYDE: Aha, so you *do* care about creatin' our own legends?

COLQUHOUN: Creatin' our own what?

MACBRYDE: The 'Two Roberts' . . . 'Colquhoun an' MacBryde' . . . we want to get into the history books, don't we?

COLQUHOUN: What you plannin' to do, shoot Wallis Simpson?

MACBRYDE: Then again, mebbe you don't believe that a couple of perfectly normal queers from the backwoods of Ayrshire have a right to take on the likes of Picasso, Braque, an' Kandinsky an' beat the livin' shit out the bastards?

COLQUHOUN: So convince me.

MACBRYDE: What d'you mean, 'convince you'? It was you that convinced *me*. D'you not remember sittin' in the life class thumbin' through the *Encyclopaedia of Modern Art* goin' 'Shite, shite, rubbish, shite . . . rubbish, rubbish, shite, shite, rubbish'?

COLQUHOUN: Mmm, vaguely. Not too sure I could muster such an informed and witty critique nowadays though.

(*Lights slowly down.* COLQUHOUN *picks up white linen jacket.*)

MACBRYDE: Light's startin' to go, Rab.

COLQUHOUN: (*Starting to cross*) Nineteen thirty-nine . . . Paul
    Nash's *English* grotesquerie 'Monster Field' is exhibited to
    reverential notices . . . Tambimuttu's 'Poetry London', a
    mixed bag of *English* trifles, gets a bung from Peter Watson,
    a 'patron of the arts' with more money than sensibility, and
    yours truly . . . a native-born *Celt* with distinct leanings
    towards the 'Ecole de Paris' as opposed to the 'Euston Road'
    mob . . . gets chucked a wad of Scottish tenners from the Art
    School to jump a cross-channel ferryboat . . .

Lights up on starry night in Italy.

MACBRYDE: (*From dark*) Robert?

COLQUHOUN: . . . Fiesole, overlooking the magical city of
    Florence . . . six weeks back I was in Spoleto, saw the Old
    Year out with the help of a half-bottle of Vecchia Romagna
    on a hilltop in Arezzo, overlooking the very landscape that
    Giotto scratched out in silverpoint . . .

MACBRYDE: (*From dark*) We still havenae found ourselves!

COLQUHOUN: . . . lost my way en route to Assisi, finished up in
    Perugia where I painted a number of portraits, including one
    of 'Due Camici Neri' which I swapped with the local padre
    for a slightly 'shop-soiled' copy of Michelangelo's sonnets
    and the address of his Nonna's *pensione* down there, next
    door to Il Duomo . . . a two-minute stroll from the Uffizi and
    a stone's throw from the very *chiesa* where Dante Alighieri
    penned the best part of his *Purgatorio* . . . which is where I
    caught buggerlugs whisperin' 'sweet *nientes*' into an olive-
    skinned altar boy's ear the other night . . .

MACBRYDE: *E! Roberto! Dove c'è?*

    (*Enter* MACBRYDE *in crumpled whites and battered panama.*)

COLQUHOUN: . . . funny, isn't it? The Arno was always there in
    Kilm–*Arno*–ck, only I never noticed till now.

    (MACBRYDE *dumps painting gear.*)

MACBRYDE: Oose, Rab.

COLQUHOUN: 'Ooserab'? What's that, ancient Etruscan for
    'Look at this strange object on ma napper'?

MACBRYDE: *Oose*, Robert . . . *oose* . . . the stuff that accumulates
    in the corners of your pockets an' the turn-ups of your

4

pantalone . . . what you an' I are goin' to be reduced to when we snuff it.

COLQUHOUN: So?

MACBRYDE: So, *cocco mio*, we've got to make certain that we're up there before that happens, right?

COLQUHOUN: Up where? As if I didnae know what he was talkin' about . . . up where?

MACBRYDE: Up there . . . (*Gazing up at stars*) . . . in the Pantheon of Painting Greats alongside Cimabue, del Sarto, Masaccio, Mantegna, Uccello, da Vinci, Bellini, Carpaccio, Verocchio . . .

COLQUHOUN: (*Suddenly*) Aaargh! Look! There: Nup, sorry, tell a lie . . . thought I spotted Pinturicchio for a second . . . carry on . . . Painting Greats . . .

MACBRYDE: On you go . . . scoff, but I've been doin' a bit of thinkin'. I've also been doin' a bit of paintin'.
(*Produces canvas on which he's painted a piazza scene.*)

COLQUHOUN: Uh huh . . .

MACBRYDE: I want you to tell me what's up with this.
(COLQUHOUN *peers closely at canvas.*)

COLQUHOUN: Just about everythin', I'd say.

MACBRYDE: C'mon, Rab, this's serious.

COLQUHOUN: The wee guy down the left-hand corner's got seven fingers on his right hand . . .

MACBRYDE: Apart from that, I'm talkin'. D'you give in?

COLQUHOUN: . . . no, hold on.

MACBRYDE: 'Reportage', Robert . . . mere 'reportage'. What you an' I's got to do is *interpret* the world around us, it's no longer enough just to paint bloody *snapshots* . . . we've go to take our lead from Joyce, right?

COLQUHOUN: 'Joyce Wright'? S'that her that does the knittin' programme on the wireless?

MACBRYDE: Quit actin' it . . . if an Irish clown with cataracts can look at the world in a different light then what's to prevent two clear-sighted Scottish geniuses from doin' likewise?

COLQUHOUN: Ah, we're *two* now, are we? This all stems from stoppin' off in Paris and scourin' the secondhand bookstalls for some trashy romance that madam here could read on the train. What do we get? *Emil and The Detectives* in the original German and a copy of *Ulysses* with the batters missin' . . . he never slept a wink all the way to Firenze. This . . . er . . . 'doin' likewise', Bobby-o?

MACBRYDE: Simple. All we do is discover a pictorial parallel to Joyce's picaresque prose, put it into practice . . . 'perfezione'.

COLQUHOUN: Aye, that's just fine and dandy, but how d'you propose . . .

MACBRYDE: Shuttup, I'm thinkin' . . .

(*Starts pacing to and fro.* COLQUHOUN *looks on for some little time as* MACBRYDE *carries on silent debate with himself.*)

COLQUHOUN: I know, I know, you all reckon *he's* the one with the savvy and I'm just the boyfriend with the good teeth and a *knack* for drawin' . . . ho!

(MACBRYDE *stops pacing.*)

You and I are Scots, right? Sprung from the loins of Finn MacCool, weaned at the paps of Jura . . . Picasso and Braque are Continentals, spoilt daft by Manet and Dada . . .

MACBRYDE: . . . Celtic 'lyricism' bonded to a European 'sensibility', we talkin'?

COLQUHOUN: . . . a Marriage Made In Heaven, Bobby.

MACBRYDE: Too pat, old son. We're lookin' to change the face of Modern Art, not to produce tit-bits for the Christmas cracker trade.

COLQUHOUN: All right, so what've *you* come up with?

MACBRYDE: . . . I'm still thinkin', dammit!

(*Starts pacing again. Lights down.*)

Lights slowly up on YOUNG ITALIAN, *elegantly dressed, admiring Uccello's 'La Battaglia' in the Uffizi. Enter Italian* FASCIST OFFICER *and German* NAZI OFFICER. *They join* YOUNG ITALIAN *in admiring painting.*

NAZI OFFICER: Ah, 'Der Kampf' . . . e veramente naturalismo, ja!

FASCIST OFFICER: Jawohl, si, e certamente wunderbar!

(*Enter* MACBRYDE, *two ice-cream cones behind his back. He joins trio admiring Renaissance masterpiece.*)

MACBRYDE: Prego.
(*Offers cone to* YOUNG ITALIAN.)
YOUNG ITALIAN: Per me?
MACBRYDE: Si.
YOUNG ITALIAN: Grazie.
MACBRYDE: I hate to break up the party, boys, but you know
what they say . . . 'Two's company' . . . why don't you
goosestep across the piazza an' impress some of the local
toddlers, I'd like a private word with Alfonso here . . .
(*He ushers* OFFICERS *away.*)
NAZI OFFICER: Idiot!
(*Exeunt.*)
MACBRYDE: (*To* YOUNG ITALIAN) . . . so where were we,
gorgeous? Aw, aye, I remember . . . we were discussin' what
happens when me an' him get back to Bonnie Scozia . . .
YOUNG ITALIAN: Dove?
MACBRYDE: . . . Scozia . . . Rabbie Burns, red puddin's, fried
dumplin' an' whisky . . . what do they learn youse chaps at
the school? Anyhow, the thing is, what's Maybole goin' to
make of my 'muckings about' with 'Modernity', an' how's
Kilmarnock goin' to cope with Roberto Colquhoun's
'cavortings' with Cubism?
YOUNG ITALIAN: Roberto chi?
MACBRYDE: Roberto Colquhoun . . . don't tell me you've never
heard of Roberto Colquhoun?
YOUNG ITALIAN: Col . . . hyooon . . .
MACBRYDE: Not Col . . . *hyooon* . . . 'Col*quhoun*'!
(*Manages to dislodge blob of ice-cream on to young Italian's
highly polished shoe.* YOUNG ITALIAN *glances down at his
besmirched footwear.*)
See . . . oh . . . ell . . . queue . . .
(*Takes grubby handkerchief from pocket, drops to his knees, and
starts wiping ice-cream from young Italian's shoe.*)
. . . you . . . aitch . . . oh . . . you . . .
(*Glances up to find* YOUNG ITALIAN *looking down at him and
licking his ice-cream cone in a provocative manner.*)
. . . saucy dago.
(*Lights slowly down.*)

7

Lights up on COLQUHOUN *in bed, smoking. A distant clock strikes three.*

Enter MACBRYDE, *shoes in hand. He tiptoes across room in dark, bumps into bed.*

MACBRYDE: Ahyah . . .

    (COLQUHOUN *snaps bedside light on.*)

COLQUHOUN: What the bloody hell time d'you call this?

MACBRYDE: I went to the Uffizi.

COLQUHOUN: You went to the Uffizi yesterday morning at ten o'clock!

MACBRYDE: I bumped into somebody.

COLQUHOUN: What 'somebody'? We don't know any 'somebodies' in Italy!

MACBRYDE: Aye, well, we do now . . . nice young chap . . . bit like thon ginger-haired boy you were pally with in the Scouts back home in Kilmarnock, remember you showed me his photograph?

COLQUHOUN: No, I don't!

MACBRYDE: His mother was a Contessa . . .

COLQUHOUN: Don't talk daft, his mother was a tobacconist.

MACBRYDE: Not the Scout, this chap I bumped into . . . she just died . . . left him a big palazzo, that's where I've been . . . spent the entire time talkin' about you an' me an' guess what happened?

COLQUHOUN: I don't have to guess . . . goodnight!

    (*Snaps light out.*)

MACBRYDE: No, listen, Rab, he's got an uncle that's got this gallery in Grenoble, handles all de Chirico's work . . .

COLQUHOUN: You know what you are, don't you?

MACBRYDE: Aye . . . your best pal an' sweetheart.

COLQUHOUN: You're a disreputable shitbag *and* a bloody liar!

MACBRYDE: No, straight up, cross ma heart an' hope to die . . . he's goin' to ask his Maw, the late Contessa, to drop this auntie, bugger, uncle a line to ask him to organize an exhibition of your paintin's . . . I've got one of their catalogues here . . . what've I done with it? I had it in the taxi . . . *bus* . . . I had it on the bus . . . you asleep, Rab?

    (*Pause.*)

8

Roberto?
(*Pause.*)
Robin?
(*Pause.*)
Robbie?
(*Pause.*)
Christ almighty, I only told this young chap you were the
greatest European painter since Pablo Picasso!
(*Bedside light snaps on.* COLQUHOUN *sits bolt upright in bed,
eyes blazing.*)

COLQUHOUN: Aye, an' I hope you also told him that *you* were the
biggest Scottish whore since Mata Hari!
(*Snaps light out. Pause.*)

MACBRYDE: (*From dark*) Mata Hari wasnae Scottish, was she?
(*Blackout.*)
(*A smack.*)
(*In blackout*) Ooooow!

Lights up. Enter COLQUHOUN *in dressing gown. He is carrying two
buff envelopes. Shells explode in middle distance.*

COLQUHOUN: January, nineteen forty . . . thanks to a *slight*
misunderstanding over the Munich Agreement, MacBryde
and I have long outstayed our welcome . . .
(*Big bang.* MACBRYDE *enters, face black, loaded down with
baggage.*)

MACBRYDE: What's the German for 'We are two Benedictine
nuns returning from the Holy Land via the Pyrenees, is this
the right train for Glasgow Queen Street?'?

COLQUHOUN: . . . Britain at War uproots, conscripts, and
generally fucks up the entire population of artists and writers
. . . back in Kilmarnock, Bobby and I receive a couple of
'billy doos' from His Majesty . . .

MACBRYDE: Uh uh, not me, chum, I'm exempted . . .
(*Offloads luggage, crosses.*)
. . . boyhood T.B.
(*Takes one envelope, rips it up.*)

COLQUHOUN: I have put myself forward as a War Artist but it's a
bit like Al Jolson applying to become the next Pope . . .

MACBRYDE: An' *you* are not goin' anywhere near any man's Army either . . .

(*Takes other envelope, rips that up.*)

. . . Can you picture Leonardo loupin' offa landin' craft an' lobbin' hand grenades at the Krauts? Course you cannae . . . and for why?

COLQUHOUN: (*Pulling on Army greatcoat*) Because he's Italian?

MACBRYDE: Because he's an *artist*, ya mug.

(*Throws torn-up pieces of envelopes into the air, from where they come down like snowflakes. Lights up on Army compound. Lights out on* MACBRYDE. COLQUHOUN *crosses.*)

COLQUHOUN: I swear to God, I've got nothin' against Herr Hitler . . . apart from his lousy watercolours. God, it's freezin' . . .

(*Blows into his hands.*)

Big chap in the bunk next to mine spent the whole of last night singin' 'We'll Meet Again' to this specky bint in a brown snapshot . . . found him hangin' from the rafters in the latrines this mornin', face was jet black.

(*Slight pause.*)

No . . . *lamp* black . . . aye, that's it, lamp black. I take back what I said about Hitler, he's a complete fuckin' bastard.

(*A low whistle.* COLQUHOUN *turns his head.* MACBRYDE *emerges from shadows, starts chucking packets over perimeter fence.*)

MACBRYDE: *Art News & Review*, five back copies . . . four Kolinsky sables . . . don't ask me what I had to do to get them . . . dozen sheets of Saunders . . . two 6B pencils . . . Christ, Rab, see tryin' to get here? Two sets of Yankee underwear, gussets're lined with parachute silk . . . how are you?

COLQUHOUN: (*Gathering up packets*) I suppose I could tell the truth and say I'm hunky-dory but he'll only fret . . . I'm bloody miserable, what d'you expect?

MACBRYDE: I did write to the War Office askin' if bein' Scottish was a 'notifiable disease' since every War Artist from Bawden to Wyndham Lewis appears to be fuckin' *English* . . . with a P.S. pointin' out that we're supposed to be *fightin'* Aryanism, not adoptin' it as a *dogma*.

COLQUHOUN: Aye, well, don't get too cheeky, *I'm* in khaki, *you're* in mufti . . . what about the shag you promised me in your letter?

MACBRYDE: Have a heart, I'm just off the train from Maybole, I doubt if I could get ma leg over this fence, never heed . . .

COLQUHOUN: *Cigarette* shag.

MACBRYDE: . . . aah. C'mere . . .

(*Squeezes small packet through mesh.*)

COLQUHOUN: You realize you could've got the Red Cross to deliver all this stuff, don't you?

MACBRYDE: C'mere, I said.

(COLQUHOUN *moves to fence, takes packet. Their lips meet through the mesh.*)

I miss you somethin' terrible, Robbie.

(*Their lips meet again.*)

CORPORAL: (*Off*) Oi, that man!

(COLQUHOUN *pulls away.*)

COLQUHOUN: Christ . . .

(*They stand blinking in the torchbeam. Enter* CORPORAL.)

CORPORAL: You filthy buggers . . .

MACBRYDE: (*Glancing over his shoulder*) He's not talkin' to us, is he?

(*Lights snap out.*)

CORPORAL: (*From blackout*) Yessah, B Company, sah . . . no sah, beg pardon, sah, but there wasn't no woman involved, sah, just a . . . 'ow shall I call it . . . a *civilian*, sah . . . that is correck, sah . . . a civilian *gent* of the same sex, sah . . . in uvver words . . . a *poof*, sah.

Lights up on MACBRYDE, *writing a letter.*

MACBRYDE: 'The Allotments, Maybole, Friday . . . My Darling Robert, just a few lines to let you know I got back safely and to find out how you are getting on. You do realize, I hope, that if it comes to a court martial you have the right to engage the services of a solicitor . . . not that it will . . . the worst they can do to you is have you gelded with a red hot bayonet and your dung funnel stitched up with hairy string. Far more outlandish things happen every day in the backcourts of

Kilmarnock . . . more outlandish than a couple of sweethearts kissing through a bloody fence, I mean, though I did hear of one young chap from Troon that had his testicles tied to the back bumper of a tramcar for shagging a tortoise but that story will keep for another time . . .

. . . the painting's going well. Peter Watson . . . you know who I mean . . . was up visiting the studios in Sauchiehall Street while I was through in Glasgow and particularly admired that still life of mine with the cantaloupes and the mincer your Mother bought off the spiv in Saltcoat . . . the "juxtaposition of the organic with the man-made" . . . his words, not mine . . . he reckoned a *breakthrough* . . .'

(*Lights up on* COLQUHOUN, *lying on top of Army bunk, letter in hand. Lights slowly down on* MACBRYDE.)

'. . . he and Cyril Connolly are starting up some magazine or other and want to do a "big splash" . . . my words, not his . . . on "Colquhoun and MacBryde" in one of their future issues. Tell me what you think so that I can . . .'

(*Enter* CORPORAL.)

CORPORAL: Right, 'Evver, on yer pins, C.O. wants a chinwag wiv yer.

(COLQUHOUN *reluctantly folds letter, swings legs off bunk.*)

Come along, come along, wot d'you fink this is, onstage at the fucking Windmill . . . jump to it, gel!

COLQUHOUN: God, he sounds just like ma Uncle Jamesie.

(*Unhooks greatcoat.*)

UNCLE JAMESIE: (*Off*) C'mon, get them crayons away an' help yur Mammy up the stair wi' that coal instead a sittin' there drawin' wee hooses like a big jessie!

COLQUHOUN: They arenae 'wee hooses', they're First Year architectural elevations, ya palooka.

UNCLE JAMESIE: (*Off*) Thur whit?

CORPORAL: If you fink that 'ow's-yer-father the uvver night qualifies you for a transfer to the Waafs you've got anuvver fink coming, sweet'eart . . . don't wax too sympaffetic to that sort of fing, our Major 'Orrocks don't . . .

UNCLE JAMESIE: (*Off*) An' whit's this yur Auld Man tells me aboot you pallin' roon wi' flamin' *nancy boys* at this bloody

Art School a yours . . . eh?

COLQUHOUN: He isnae a 'nancy boy', he's an *artist*.

UNCLE JAMESIE: (*Off*) *Artist*, ma fanny . . . yur Auld Man's awready goat flang oot the Boolin' Club 'cos folk ur talkin'.

CORPORAL: Last shirtlifter wot managed to slip froo the net 'ad 'er little winkle cut off an' nailed to the cook'ouse door by one of the lads in C Company . . .

UNCLE JAMESIE: (*Off*) *Nancy boy!*

CORPORAL: . . . wouldn't like that to 'appen to us now, would we, 'Evver?

COLQUHOUN: (*Smiling*) No, Corp.

CORPORAL: Right, let's be 'aving you! Hup, two, free, four . . . hup, two, free, four . . .
(*Marches* COLQUHOUN *off. Lights snap out.*)
(*From blackout*) Less rabbit in the ranks! Right wheel! Hup, two, free, four . . . *right* wheel, I said! Don't none of you lot compre'end the King's fucking English? Stand to attention, that man!

Lights up on pile of mailbags centre-stage. COLQUHOUN, *sleeves rolled up, wipes his brow.*

COLQUHOUN: Twenty-eight days 'confined to barracks' . . . C.O. was convinced I was trying to 'work my ticket', refused to accept the Corporal's eye-witness account of 'gross indecency', put me on 'camp fatigues' . . . how's about that for poetic injustice?

UNCLE JAMESIE: (*Off*) Away, ya bloody *nancy boy!*
(COLQUHOUN *heaves mailbag on to his shoulder. Enter* CORPORAL.)

CORPORAL: (*Over shoulder to unseen unit*) Eyes front, that man! Anuvver crack and I'll 'ave you up in front of the C.O. before you can say 'Lift Up Your Kilts' . . .
(*To* COLQUHOUN) . . . 'Ell's bells, Vera, s'that all you've shifted?

COLQUHOUN: Give us a chance, Corp, they're bloody heavy.

CORPORAL: 'Bloody 'eavy'? 'Bloody . . .'? I should bloody well fink they are 'bloody 'eavy', they're stuffed to the fucking gunnels wiv personal bloody love letters from wives and

bloody sweet'earts to their loved ones at the bloody Front . . .
somefink you wouldn't know nuffink about, you bloody
moron . . . now, get a bloody move on!
(*Propels* COLQUHOUN *forward with boot.* COLQUHOUN
staggers, falls, lies still.)
Oh, yuss . . . 'ighly bloody comical and I don't fink. 'Oo 'asn't
been eating 'er porridge then? Eh? 'Oo 'asn't been . . .
(*Breaks off.*)
. . . 'ere, you awlright, Princess?
(*Bends over* COLQUHOUN.)
Oh, my Gawd . . .
(*Loudly.*) . . . that man! Leg it across to the M.O.'s 'ut and tell
'im to get out 'ere double quick, we got a pansy wiv the
dropsy. 'Urry up, jump to it!
(*To* COLQUHOUN) Tell you one fing, darlin', you do not suit
that blue lipstick.
(*Lights down.*)

Lights up on MACBRYDE, *leafing through* Horizon, *tearing out pages,*
fixing them to wall with drawing pins.

MACBRYDE: (*Sings*) Oh, we're riding along on the crest of a wave,
the sun is in the sky . . . all our eyes on the distant *Horizon* . . .
look out for passers-by . . . we'll go sailing when other ships
are under hailing, we're riding along on the crest of a wave . . .
(*Lights up on* COLQUHOUN, *wrapped in blanket, recuperating.*)
COLQUHOUN: (*Over* MACBRYDE'S *singing*) Quack diagnosed
angina, ordered complete peace and quiet . . .
MACBRYDE: . . . aaargh!
COLQUHOUN: . . . some bloody hope. What is it now?
MACBRYDE: Listen to this, Rab . . .
(*Reads.*)
'. . . as to the other Robert' . . . that's you . . . 'the sombre
figures of his great paintings . . . "Woman With Leaping
Cat", "The Whistle Seller", "The Dubliners" . . . so skilfully
combine the tragic and the noble that his assertion about the
human condition approaches a dramatic grandeur that
elevates his art head and shoulders above that of his
contemporaries'!

COLQUHOUN: (*Weakly*) Aye, very nice . . .
    (*Reaches out and turns radio on.*)
MACBRYDE: What d'you mean, 'very nice'? I've just read you out
    the best review you've ever had an' all you can say is . . .
COLQUHOUN: Shh, listen.
MACBRYDE: Listen what?
COLQUHOUN: Shh!
MACBRYDE: What?
    (*Bring up chimes of Big Ben on radio.*)
COLQUHOUN: Happy Nineteen Forty-two, Bobby.
MACBRYDE: Yahoo!
    (*Reaches across and embraces* COLQUHOUN. *Scottish country
    dance music bursts forth from radio.*)
    Right, you, up.
    (*Hauls* COLQUHOUN *on to floor and into dance.*)
COLQUHOUN: Christ sake, what you doin', I've got a bad heart!
MACBRYDE: You want to be fit for London, don't you? Hyoooch!
    (*Whirls* COLQUHOUN *round and round.*)
COLQUHOUN: What you talkin' about, 'London'?
MACBRYDE: Peter Watson's got us a studio! Eeeeeehah!
COLQUHOUN: What!
MACBRYDE: Bedford Gardens, Notting Hill . . . d'you think
    you'll manage six flights of stairs with your 'bad . . .
COLQUHOUN: Aaaargh!
    (COLQUHOUN'*s face contorts in agony, he collapses like a sack
    of mail.*)
MACBRYDE: . . . aw, my God, your heart, Robert!
    (*Drops to his knees over* COLQUHOUN.)
COLQUHOUN: Ma heart nothin', I just stood on one of your stupit
    drawin' pins! Oooow!
    (*Prises 'drawing pin' from big toe.*)
MACBRYDE: Ya pig! Don't you dare give me a fright like that ever
    again, d'you hear!
    (*Smacks* COLQUHOUN *on the head.*)
COLQUHOUN: Ahyah!
    (*Clutches his head.*)
MACBRYDE: Gimme that.
    (*Grabs* COLQUHOUN'*s injured foot, sticks big toe in his mouth.*)

COLQUHOUN: Ah, ah, ah, ah . . .
   (MACBRYDE *withdraws toe, examines it.*)
MACBRYDE: Pull yourself together, man, it's only a tiny wee
   prick.
   (*They look at each other.*)
COLQUHOUN/MACBRYDE: (*Together*) Aye, I know, but it'll do a
   turn till 'Mr Right' comes along.
COLQUHOUN: C'mere, ya cheeky bastard.
   (*Hauls* MACBRYDE *to his feet. They embrace.*)
   I'm so happy, Bobby.
MACBRYDE: Me too, Rab. Me too.
   (*Bring up Jack Buchanan's version of 'Dancing Cheek To
   Cheek' as* COLQUHOUN *and* MACBRYDE *take off into dance.*)

Lights up on Bedford Gardens studio.
COLQUHOUN: (*Gazing out over night-time London*) Seventy-seven
   Bedford Gardens, Notting Hill . . . an unlikely locus for
   'Paradise Found' but that is surely where we are . . .
   (*Turning. Loudly.*) . . . you were right, pal, it really is.
   Heaven, I mean.
   (*Enter* MACBRYDE *with furniture. Hands lighted candle to*
   COLQUHOUN.)
MACBRYDE: D'you want me to leave the eyes in or squeeze them
   out into the sink for a puddin'?
COLQUHOUN: Come again?
   (MACBRYDE *sets pieces of furniture down, recrosses to exit.*)
MACBRYDE: Squeeze them out, I reckon . . . there's some custard
   powder in one of the suitcases . . .
   (*Exits to reappear carrying sheep's head in brown paper
   wrapping.*)
   . . . your favourite . . . sheep's heid goulash.
   (*Loud banging on door.*)
   That'll be some of the 'Welcoming Committee'. . .
   (*Recrossing to door. Loudly.*) . . . coming!
   (*Throws door open to discover irate* ARP WARDEN *on landing.*)
ARP WARDEN: Are these your apartments?
MACBRYDE: No, he's just passin' through . . .
   (*To sheep's head*) . . . aren't you, son?

(*Sotto voce to* ARP WARDEN) Don't, whatever you do,
mention 'goulash', I told him we were just havin' 'drinks'.
COLQUHOUN: Who is it, Robert?
ARP WARDEN: (*Angrily*) Get that flaming light out in there!
MACBRYDE: (*Over shoulder*) Aye, get that flamin' light out, what
are you, blind or somethin', the skies are thick with bloody
Heinkels!
(COLQUHOUN *blows candles out.*)
(*To* ARP WARDEN) Accept my apologies, sergeant, but my
compadre lost his sight in a tragic painting accident not that
long back . . . poked his eye out with a copyin' ink pencil,
I've brung him down from Bonnie Scotland to run his fingers
over the Rembrandts in the Wallace Collection, would you
care to stay for some goulash?
(*To sheep's head*) I didnae say that.
ARP WARDEN: If I have to call here again you could find yourself
facing a stiff one, m'lad.
MACBRYDE: (*Over shoulder*) D'you hear that, Robert? Hardly two
hours in the Big Smoke an' already we're gettin' offers.
ARP WARDEN: Next time I'll be accompanied by a police
constable. Goodnight.
(*Turns to go.*)
MACBRYDE: You couldnae make it a matelot, could you?
ARP WARDEN: (*Under his breath*) Bloody queers . . .
MACBRYDE: Fuckin' nosy parker . . .
(*Exit* ARP WARDEN. COLQUHOUN *relights candles.*
MACBRYDE *crosses to screened-off scullery.*)
COLQUHOUN: How long d'you think we should give it?
MACBRYDE: About four hours at a low peep.
COLQUHOUN: Not the goulash, gettin' ourselves a gallery, I'm
talkin'.
MACBRYDE: Now, there you have me, Rab . . .
(*Another knock at the door.* MACBRYDE *stops.*)
. . . but hold hard, who's this? Is it the Hanover, the
Redfern, Delbanco, Grabowski . . .?
COLQUHOUN: It'll be that bloody warden back.
(*Blows candle out.* MACBRYDE *crosses to door, opens it.* JANKEL
ADLER, *the Polish artist, enters. He is wearing a boiler suit and*

17

flat cap, a galvanized bucket in his hand.)

MACBRYDE: What one are you?

ADLER: Naw, naw, zis is *my* kvestion . . . if you are Culwhoon zer
is just a chance . . . if you are ze uzzer vun zen ve are fucked.
Here, I brung you some beer.

(*Hands bucket to* MACBRYDE.)

MACBRYDE: Who *is* this?

ADLER: (*To* COLQUHOUN) Adler . . . Jankel Adler . . . I used to
have a wee room and kitchen stoodio in Glesca, I am now up
ze stairs here . . . don't vorry about getting ze bucket back to
me, I now hev ze inside lavatry.

(COLQUHOUN *relights candles.*)

You know vot Picasso once said to me?

MACBRYDE: Somethin' like 'Piss off, ya Polish upstart', only in
Spanish. Here . . . we don't want your lousy beer.

(*Hands bucket back to* ADLER, *crosses to scullery.* COLQUHOUN
cuts him off.)

COLQUHOUN: (*Sotto voce*) What you playin' at, ya mug? This guy
used to share a studio with Paul Klee!

MACBRYDE: I don't care if he shared his last gasper with Groucho
Marx, what does he mean '. . . if you are ze uzzer vun ve are
fucked'?

COLQUHOUN: (*Sotto voce*) He's just tryin' to be fuckin' sociable!
(*To* ADLER) Sorry, you were sayin'?

(MACBRYDE *disappears into scullery with sheep's head.*)

Here, let me take that.

(*Takes beer bucket from* ADLER.)

ADLER: 'Jankel,' he said . . . 'you are a big talent, do not vaste
your time viz piglets.'

COLQUHOUN: 'Piglets'?

ADLER: '. . . pygmies . . . do not vaste your time viz pygmies.' Zis
is good adwise, naw?

MACBRYDE: (*From scullery*) Naw, he's a shortarsed wee cunt,
Picasso . . . why don't you blow, whatever-your-name is?

COLQUHOUN: Just ignore him, he's a shortarsed wee cunt,
MacBryde . . .

(*Loudly*) . . . just you get on with makin' that goulash.

ADLER: Ah, I am very tasty for goulash ven I zink of Poland.

MACBRYDE: (*From scullery*) Well, think about somethin' else, pal, you're not gettin' any.

COLQUHOUN: Shuttup, Robert.

(*To* ADLER) He's not usually this touchy . . .

MACBRYDE: (*From scullery*) Aye, I fuckin' am!

(*Great deal of banging and thumping from scullery.*)

ADLER: I have seen your vork in Connolly's magazine . . . it is werry goot but it needs to be tougher . . . feel zat. (*Flexes bicep.*) Forged in adwersity, tempered in extremis. You hev to be strongk to produce strongk art. Vot you require is '*iron*', Culwhoon . . .

MACBRYDE: (*From scullery*) Shite . . .

(*Emerging with sheep's head in pot*) . . . bloody gas's went out. (*To* ADLER) You wouldnae care to follow its example, would you?

(*A knock at the door.*)

COLQUHOUN: I'll get it . . .

(*To* MACBRYDE *in passing*) . . . you're gettin' sent to your bed if you don't behave yourself.

(*Opens door. There, swaying drunkenly on the landing, is the baby-faced* DYLAN THOMAS *in a three-piece corduroy suit, an almost empty half-bottle in his hand.*)

DYLAN: (*Slightly slurred*)

> Before I knocked and flesh let enter
> With liquid hands tapped on the womb,
> I who was shapeless as the water
> That shaped the Jordan near my home
> Was brother to Mnetha's daughter
> And sister to the fatherless worm . . .

(*Hiccups.*) . . . I bring you greetings from the denizens of Fitzrovia, dear boy.

MACBRYDE: Sorry, sweetheart, the only people we know cried 'Dennison' come from Dalry . . . wouldnae recognize 'Fitzrovia' if you put it on a plate with a fried egg on top. Right, hands up who wants some delicious *raw* sheep's heid goulash?

DYLAN: Oh, Christ . . . 'scuse me . . .

(*Stumbles past* COLQUHOUN, *staggers across the room, hand*

over his mouth, sticks his head into beer bucket, throws up.
COLQUHOUN, MACBRYDE, *and* ADLER *look on as he comes up for air, eyes closed, face deathly pale, and keels over on to the floor and lies still.*)

MACBRYDE: (*Bending over* DYLAN) Ho . . . 'scuse me – yoohoo . . . wakey, wakey . . . you couldnae see your way to lendin' us a shillin' for the gas, could you? Ho . . . stupit appearance?

COLQUHOUN: Try Jankel.

MACBRYDE: Good idea.
(*To* DYLAN) Ho . . . 'scuse me . . . *Jankel* . . . yoohoo . . . (*No response. To* COLQUHOUN) . . . nup, doesnae seem to be workin', Robert. Aw, *him* Jankel?
(*To* ADLER) Any loose change for the goulash, *Jankel*?
(*To* COLQUHOUN) So, how come you an' him's on first name terms, s'there somethin' you're not tellin' me, Colquhoun?

COLQUHOUN: Aye, very droll.

ADLER: (*Producing small handful of change*) All I got's a handfulla vashers, ze English are such Frankensteins, zey don't vish to buy paintings.

DYLAN: (*Coming round*) I think someone better fetch me a taxicab . . . (*Produces ten bob note.*)

MACBRYDE: Thanks.
(*Plucks ten shilling note from* DYLAN'*s hand.*)

COLQUHOUN: That will not go into the gas meter, Robert.

MACBRYDE: No, but it *will* go into the drinks kitty.
(*Hands pot to* COLQUHOUN.)
What d'you say to a nice bottle of Old Jamaica rum with your goulash?

DYLAN: Oh, God . . .
(*Hangs his head over beer bucket.* MACBRYDE *crosses to door.*)

MACBRYDE: Try pumpin' some more puerile pap about Picasso out wur Polish pal while I pop downstairs, Robert.
(*Exits whistling.*)

COLQUHOUN: I wouldn't pay too much heed to Robert, his own Mother couldnae thole him.

ADLER: (*Leafing through canvases*) Don't vorry, Culwhoon, I am vell used to being ridikooled by ze moderately talented . . .

ah, zese are goot, I like . . . (*Pulls out several canvases*) . . .
ven are you painting zese vuns?

COLQUHOUN: I'm not, they're his.

ADLER: I'm zorry?

COLQUHOUN: Those were painted by the 'moderately talented',
mine are over there.

ADLER: Ah.

DYLAN: (*Searching pockets*) What the hell have I done with that
ten bob note? I'm almost positive I had a ten bob note
somewhere . . .

(*Loud, overlapping banging at door.*)

COLQUHOUN: Shite.

(*Blows candle out.*)

DYLAN: (*On hands and knees*) Buggeration.

(*Feels about floor in the dark for missing ten bob note. More loud
banging at door.*)

COLQUHOUN: Aye, all right, I'm comin', I'm comin'.

(*Crosses, throws door open.* GEORGE BARKER, *the poet, steps
inside, removes hat, hands it to* COLQUHOUN. *Glances furtively
back down the stairs.*)

BARKER: Thought I'd managed to shake her off in Denmark
Street, turns up on the poxy fucking bus . . .

(*Removes filthy raincoat.*) . . . Antwerp, couple of years back,
ugly fucking bitch . . . (*Catches sight of sheep's head in pot.*)
. . . good Christ, that could be her twin sister. Adler, you old
fucker, good to see you . . .

(*Chucks raincoat into a corner. To* COLQUHOUN) . . . don't tell
me, let me guess . . . you're one of The Roberts, right?
George Barker, welcome to Babylon . . .

DYLAN: Barker! What the devil are you doing here? Last I heard
you were in America *hacking* out some ditties for lots of
dollars . . . let me have a look at you . . .

(*Staggers across the room, arms outstretched.*) . . . my dear boy!
(BARKER *neatly sidesteps at the last moment.* DYLAN *goes
stumbling out on to landing.* COLQUHOUN *shuts the door. Loud
crash and yelling as* DYLAN *goes tumbling downstairs. Silence.*)

BARKER: (*Smiling*) . . . one less *slim volume* in the offing. Johnny
Minton sends his apologies, he's up in Kinloch-fucking-

somewhere with the Pioneer Corps, instructed me to act as his 'emissary' . . . interesting piece in Connolly's rag, you must've been flattered . . .

COLQUHOUN: Aye, we were quite pleased.

BARKER: . . . complete load of fucking tosh, of course.

(*Crossing towards beer bucket.*)

COLQUHOUN: I beg your pardon?

BARKER: Johnny Tonge, chap that wrote you up . . . can't tell his Arp from his Ensor as far as I can make out but it may help you sell a couple of your little pictures . . . is this some of your famous 'home brew' here, Jankel?

COLQUHOUN: (*Setting goulash pot down*) Aye, let me get you a glass.

(*Picks up tumbler, dips it into bucket, scoops up 'carroty' beer.*)

BARKER: Managed to dodge a doodlebug in Drury Lane, blew some old bag under a fucking fire engine, could do with a drink . . . cheers.

(*Takes glass from* COLQUHOUN, *swigs thirstily. Freezes.*)

ADLER: If you don't care for ze carrots spit zem on to ze floor.

COLQUHOUN: (*Picking up goulash pot*) Aye, like fuck . . . here, spit them into the goulash.

(BARKER *stands rigidly, hand clapped over his mouth, unsure whether to swallow or puke. The door flies open.* MACBRYDE *appears, bottle in one hand,* DYLAN, *bloody-nosed, hanging on to him.*)

You took your time . . . where'd you go for the rum, Tobago?

(MACBRYDE *eyes* BARKER, *still frozen, with suspicion.*)

MACBRYDE: Goin' to open that, Django?

(*Passes rum bottle to* ADLER.)

DYLAN: (*Holding head back to prevent blood dripping*) You'll find a sheet of blotting paper in one of the pockets . . . came with the suit, didn't it?

(MACBRYDE *helps him across to bed.* ADLER *hunts around for something to open bottle with.*)

COLQUHOUN: This's George Barker, he's a poet.

MACBRYDE: I know he's a poet, I'm just after carryin' him up the stairs.

(*Dumps* DYLAN *on bed.*)

COLQUHOUN: Not him . . . *him.*

MACBRYDE: Him who, him there?

ADLER: I need a screwcork for zis . . .

MACBRYDE: (*To* COLQUHOUN) What'd you say his name was?

COLQUHOUN: George Barker.

> (*Ferries goulash pot into scullery.* ADLER *trails after him with unopened rum bottle.*)

MACBRYDE: (*To* BARKER) Me an' Robert's goin' to be makin' an assault on Bond Street shortly, might be worth a clutch of 'heroic couplets', Georgie Boy.

> (COLQUHOUN *re-emerges from scullery.* ADLER *follows him out.*)

COLQUHOUN: Did you get some change for the gas?

MACBRYDE: Does he talk English, d'you know?

> (*Loudly, to* BARKER) Spot of rum, *Georgie Boy*?
> (*Takes unopened bottle of rum from* ADLER, *smashes the neck off, pours rum into mugs.* BARKER'*s resolve goes.*)

BARKER: Bleagh!

> (*He spews 'carroty' beer on to floor.*)
> Don't call me fucking 'Georgie Boy', the name's *Barker.*

MACBRYDE: Fine. Good to meet you, Barker.

> (*Sticks out a hand. Smiles broadly and openly.*)

BARKER: Thank you very much. (*Takes hold of outstretched hand.*) How d'you . . .?

> (*Breaks off, realizing too late that* MACBRYDE *has placed a piece of broken bottle in his hand.* BARKER *stares down at his bleeding palm.* MACBRYDE *gives a chuckle.*)

COLQUHOUN: (*Quietly*) Shit.

BARKER: You bastard.

> (*He brings his injured hand up smartly and belts* MACBRYDE *across the ear, leaving a bloody handprint on the side of his face.* MACBRYDE *carries on smiling. Lets smile fade. Pause.*)

ADLER: Right, zat's got ze 'niceties' out ze road, who's for a snifter? Culwhoon?

> (*Passes mug to* COLQUHOUN.)

COLQUHOUN: All the best.

ADLER: Barker . . .

(*Passes mug to* BARKER. BARKER *accepts it silently.* ADLER *offers a third mug to* MACBRYDE. MACBRYDE *carries on staring at* BARKER.)

COLQUHOUN: Drink, Robert?

MACBRYDE: No, I'm fine, thanks. Down the hatch . . .
(*Lifts cut hand above his head and lets the blood drip into his open mouth. Give a gurgling laugh.*)

DYLAN: (*Sitting up on bed*) I'll have whatever he's having, only make it a double, there's a good chap.
(*Lights slowly down. Bring up jumbled laughter, chatter, party noise. Fade to black.*)
(COLQUHOUN *steps forward into his light.*)

COLQUHOUN: Last thing I recall is MacBryde performing an improvised 'pas de deux' with a big wumman in plus fours . . . stark bollock naked. Not a sight I would readily recommend to those of a queasy disposition . . .
(*Enter* MACBRYDE *with two tumblers.*)

MACBRYDE: (*Brightly*) Some night.

COLQUHOUN: Some goulash. God . . .

MACBRYDE: Some medicine. Here.
(*Hands* COLQUHOUN *a tumbler.*)
So what was *Jankel* sayin'? You an' him spent the best part of the night shoutin' at each other like you were bosom buddies from 'way back when.

COLQUHOUN: He was exhortin' us to plumb our Celtic roots and resist at all costs becoming ersatz Englishmen.

MACBRYDE: Quite right, I thought you were becomin' a wee bit anglified.

COLQUHOUN: What're you talkin' about?

MACBRYDE: Your pinky's stickin' out.
(COLQUHOUN *tucks his little finger round the tumbler.*)

COLQUHOUN: Is it fuck.

MACBRYDE: What else was he sayin'?

COLQUHOUN: He wants to provide me with some 'iron'.

MACBRYDE: Well, he can just fuck off, *I'll* provide you with 'iron', there's a Timothy White's at the corner . . . get you a big tin of 'jelloids', then it's 'Cork Street, here we come', right?

COLQUHOUN: You don't think we should wait till we've done some
    new work, no?
MACBRYDE: You mean, new *'English'* work? No, I fuckin' don't,
    Rab. Ferguson's just started up 'The New Scottish Group' in
    Glasgow, they're sayin' it's in the vanguard of the Neo-
    Romantic movement, d'you want a buncha neds from North
    of the Border to get the better of Colquhoun an' MacBryde?
COLQUHOUN: Not on your fuckin' nellie.
    (*They exeunt in opposite directions. Lights out.*)

Lights up on Cork Street. COLQUHOUN *and* MACBRYDE *enter from
opposite directions, each with a bunch of canvases under his arm.*
COLQUHOUN: Right, you take that side and I'll take this one, we'll
    meet up at the end of the street and toss a coin to decide what
    lucky gallery gets to show us, right?
MACBRYDE: (*Loudly*) D'you hear that, ya buggers? Stand by for
    the biggest shock wave to hit London since Charles Edward
    Stuart turned back at Peterborough. Right, go!
    (*Music. They dodge in and out of galleries, becoming less
    exuberant and more dejected as they get turned down by each of the
    galleries in turn, till at last they reach the end of the street.*)
    Buck up, Rab, everybody knows they're a buncha card-
    carryin' Philistines that couldnae tell a *real* paintin' if it fell
    into their mock turtle soup.
    (*Loudly*) Eejits! Wankers! Cunts!
    (*To* COLQUHOUN) Just as well I don't let these things upset
    me. C'mon, you can buy me a pint.
COLQUHOUN: What with? We havenae any fuckin' money.
MACBRYDE: (*Loudly*) Bastards!
COLQUHOUN: I told you we should've waited . . .
    (*Puts his foot through canvas in disgust.*)
MACBRYDE: Aw, that's very clever, that is. Why don't you destroy
    the whole bloody lot of them . . . on you go, it wasnae ma fault
    they didnae like us! You could've combed your hair an' put on
    a clean shirt, I left one out for you, but, aw, no, you want to
    play at the fuckin' 'bohemian' . . . that's probably what put
    them off us, d'you realize that? Come to think about it, I got
    several offers to show *ma* pictures, I wish to Christ I'd . . .

25

COLQUHOUN: Aw, shuttup.

(*Smashes canvas over* MACBRYDE's *head.* MACBRYDE *stands there 'framed'.* COLQUHOUN *starts to laugh.*)

MACBRYDE: It isnae funny, Rab.

COLQUHOUN: Aye, it is . . . laugh, ya bastard . . . laugh when you're told!

(*Sticks his face close to* MACBRYDE's, *neither of them laughing. Lights down.*)

Lights up on Bedford Gardens. COLQUHOUN *wanders on, pausing in front of cheval glass. Takes a pipe from his pocket, clenches it between his teeth. Poses.*

COLQUHOUN: 'Self Portrait, Notting Hill, Summer, Nineteen Forty-three' . . . a suitably serious image though not entirely devoid of humorous undertones . . . a hint of self-mockery without overdoing it.

(*Thinking twice about pipe before junking it.*)

I am a serious, even solemn personality . . . cross out 'personality', substitute 'character' . . . uh uh, caught a whiff of the greasepaint there . . . revert to 'personality' . . . a solemn personality . . . fuck it, Tommy Handley's a 'personality', just stick to 'artist', what's good enough for Pinturicchio is good enough for you, pal . . . a serious *artist* . . . an artist to be taken seriously, given his due . . . *recognized* even . . . 'Make it with love and keep it simple' . . . not too mawkish, no? No. Fine. Colquhoun and MacBryde, after something of a false start, are now on target . . . excellent!

(*Exits.*)

(*Enter* MACBRYDE. *He is wearing a fisherman's jersey, bow tie, and kilt. He is in his socks, a parcel under his arm. He turns this way and that in mirror.*)

MACBRYDE: Not bad . . . not bad. 'Self Portrait In Highland Rigout, High Summer, Forty-three' . . . a tantalizingly decadent image but one not wholly bereft of serious sub-text . . . solemnity, even. A playful, though solemn character . . . an artist . . . and here I quote . . . whose 'winning waywardness' hides a deeply serious personality . . . aye,

26

that's it . . . we'll show the bastards . . . the Two Roberts,
Colquhoun and MacBryde, following a somewhat sticky
take-off, are fast hurtling towards oblivion, fuck!
(*Enter* COLQUHOUN, *a parcel under his arm. Stops. After a few
seconds,* MACBRYDE *becomes aware of his presence.*)
Well . . . what d'you think?
(COLQUHOUN *just stares at him.*)
Listen, Rab, after what happened that last time we ain't
takin' any chances, we've got to play it to the hilt . . . charm
the buggers.
(*Pause.*)
Awright, scrub 'charm', we've got to *intrigue* them, right?
(*Pause.*)
Forget 'intrigue', I never mentioned 'intrigue', let's just
fascinate them, eh? I mean, what could possibly be more
fascinatin' than a Scotchman on the make?
(*Pause.*)
You're not listenin', Robert . . . I said, what could be more
fascinatin' than . . .
COLQUHOUN: (*Lets parcel fall open to reveal kilt*) *Two* Scotchmen!
MACBRYDE: Ya bloody . . .
COLQUHOUN: . . . hypocrite? Ah, not so, bonnie lad . . . not so.
Since the fuckers havenae a bloody clue what constitutes a
good painting, we've got to help them along . . . harmonizes
perfectly sweetly with that original stratagem you found 'too
pat' . . . a sophisticated cocktail of the louche and the lyrical,
the cheeky and the sublime, the . . .
(*Breaks off.*)
(MACBRYDE *has unwrapped pair of two-tone 'golfing shoes' and
is putting them on.*)
MACBRYDE: (*Glancing up*) What? (*Glancing down*) Aw, these?
Pretty snazzy, huh? Cut them down out an old pair of your
Army boots . . . astonishin' what the bread knife and a lick of
oil paint can accomplish, innit?
(COLQUHOUN *turns away, lets kilt fall to the floor.*)
S'up?
COLQUHOUN: (*Crossing to look out*) Mebbe it isn't such a brilliant
wheeze, after all.

MACBRYDE: What you talkin' about? A coupla minutes back you
were positively . . . wait a mo, penny's dropped, it's the
shoes, right?

COLQUHOUN: No, no, s'nothing to do with the shoes.

MACBRYDE: It is so the fucking shoes, you were perfectly
enthusiastic up till you clocked the footgear . . . come off, ya
pigs!
(*Struggles to get shoes off.*)

COLQUHOUN: You see what I'm up against?
(MACBRYDE *chucks offending footwear across the room.*)

MACBRYDE: Happy now? I'll walk about in ma bare feet, catch
ma death of pneumonia, how does that suit you?

COLQUHOUN: What you talkin' about, it's the bloody summer,
it's roastin' out there.

MACBRYDE: Aw, shut your face, ya miserable bastard!
(*Pause.*)

COLQUHOUN: C'mon, get them back on . . . (*Gathers up golfing
shoes*) . . . here.

MACBRYDE: Away to fuck, *you* get them on.

COLQUHOUN: *Me?* You must be jokin', pal, I wouldnae be caught
dead in these stupit-lookin' items.

MACBRYDE: Aye, but it's awright for me to wear them, is that it?
Thanks a bloody million!

COLQUHOUN: Aw, for God's sake . . . no, it is not awright for you
to wear them, that's what we're talkin' about, ya stupit cunt
. . . I can see us walkin' into some fancy gallery and askin'
them to look at our work and all *they* can look at is *your*
ludicrous, home-made fuckin' *golfin'* shoes!

MACBRYDE: Aw, it's *fancy* galleries we're tryin' to get into now, is
it? An' those are not '*golfin'* shoes, they're perfectly normal,
straightforward, everyday footwear!

COLQUHOUN: Ha!

MACBRYDE: What d'you mean, 'Ha!'? When was the last time
you spotted a golfer wearin' shoes like them, you havenae!
(*Lights start going down.* COLQUHOUN *picks up kilt, heads for
exit.*)
If there's one thing I can't abide it's a moanin' fuckin'
Minnie! They're a work of *art*, them shoes . . . if Dali

28

cobbled them bastards they'd be in the fuckin' Prado!
'*Golfin*'' shoes . . . I'll give you fuckin' 'golfin'' shoes! An
entire generation of MacBrydes fell at the Battle of Flodden
in *exactly* that footwear an' if you say 'Hell mend them' I'll
fuckin' batter you! Two-tone *brogues*, that's what they are
. . . two-tone Highland brogues, ya bastard!

Lights up on Soho street. COLQUHOUN *enters, his nose buried in
paper bag.*
COLQUHOUN: (*Almost to himself*) Chrome Yellow, Lemon Yellow,
    Raw Sienna, Purple Brown . . . Burnt Umber, Prussian
    Blue, Venetian Red, Roasted Ivory, Lapis Lazuli . . .
    (COLQUHOUN *is wearing the kilt.*)
    . . . Terre Verte, Veridian, Van Dyke Brown, Rose Madder,
    Cadmium Orange, Hooker's Green, Mahogany Lake . . .
    (*Enter* MACBRYDE, *still in kilt, a small parcel behind hs back.*
    COLQUHOUN *looks up from paper bag.*)
    Well?
MACBRYDE: There's plenty other pawnshops, Rab.
COLQUHOUN: Aye.
    (*Scrunches up bag of imaginary 'paints', tosses it over his
    shoulder.*)
MACBRYDE: Don't fret, I've just spied a ten shillin' note headin'
    this way, don't look.
    (*Enter* GEORGE BARKER *on the other side of the street.*)
    Don't look, I said!
    (*Waving*) Ho . . . Blood Brother?
BARKER: Good grief . . . (*Crosses.*)
    . . . couldn't decide between a couple of local tarts drumming
    up business or a pair of old slags wandered in off Shaftesbury
    Avenue following a matinee performance of 'Miracle In The
    Gorbals' . . . bit *avant garde* even for these parts, don't you
    think?
    (MACBRYDE *unwraps parcel, displays 'golfing' shoes.*)
    . . . I've said it once, I'll say it again . . . good grief.
COLQUHOUN: How's the mitt? That went down well.
MACBRYDE: Go nice with that outfit you're sportin', Blood
    Brother . . . all your heterosexual poets are takin' up golf this

year, cannae think why, I've always regarded it as a *man's* game, maself . . . look, you can just make out Bobby Jones's initials burnt into the welt . . . 'W.D.' . . . see? Let you have them for thirty bob, how's that?

BARKER: I've got a better idea . . . why don't I take the pair of you to the Colony Club, get pissed as fucking arseholes, introduce you to my great chum, Muriel?

MACBRYDE: You're on.

(*Hands 'golfing' shoes to* COLQUHOUN.)

COLQUHOUN: What about this list of colours we need?

MACBRYDE: What we *need* right now, Robert, is a good bucket. C'mon, the Blood Brother's forkin' out for the fire-water . . .

BARKER: (*Wandering on ahead*) Come along, you pair, if we don't get a move on all the bloody pubs'll be open, spoil the bloody fun of it.

MACBRYDE: (*To* COLQUHOUN) Please yourself . . . (*Loudly*) . . . hold your horses, Georgie Boy . . .

(*Linking arms with* BARKER) Don't wait up for us, Robert.

(*Exeunt. Lights slowly down on* COLQUHOUN.)

Lights up on Colony Club. MURIEL BELCHER, *a handsome woman with aristocratic bearing, is perched on one of the leopardskin bar stools, smoking.*

Enter BARKER *and* MACBRYDE.

MURIEL: Hullo, cunty, you still owe me for two large gins and a bottle of Guinness. If you don't stump up you're fucking barred, who's this little poppet?

(*To* MACBRYDE) What can I get you, dear?

MACBRYDE: (*Sourly*) I'll have a whisky.

MURIEL: Oh, Gawd, she's a Scotchman . . .

(*To* BARKER) What line is she in, dear? Hasn't got the legs for a chorus gel . . . hideous profile, reminds me of a particularly heinous-looking beaverette . . . I'd have her put down if I were you . . .

(*To* MACBRYDE) . . . what make of whisky, dear? We've got a nice one from Nova Scotia and a not-so-nice one from upstairs . . .

(*Loudly*) . . . Carmel? Are we in our boudoir, dear? Well, get

your backside off my fucking bed and fetch down two large
whiskies, one for me, one for Miss Scotland . . . she looks
like she could do with one.

(*To* BARKER) Now, dear, what's your pleasure? And if you
say having a grope at Carmel when she comes downstairs
you're out in the fucking street.

BARKER: Muriel, I'd like you to meet Robert MacBryde . . .
Robert and I are 'Blood Brothers' . . .

MURIEL: That's nice, dear, so who's shagging who?
(*Lights snap out.*)

Lights up on Bedford Gardens. COLQUHOUN *seated morosely in front
of easel, staring at canvas. A loud groan from outside. Enter*
MACBRYDE *very slowly, clutching his head.*

COLQUHOUN: So, tell me.

MACBRYDE: Tell you what? Aw, God . . .
Don't rush me, Rab, ma brain feels like a two-
hundredweight pickled walnut squashed inside a bee's
kneecap . . .
(*Cluthes head.*)
. . . God, never again.

COLQUHOUN: 'Never again'? *I* sat up till a quarter to four waitin'
for you to come back, what happens? You're too bloody
moroculous to blurt out more than 'We've knocked it off . . .
The Great Idea' before curlin' up behind the door an' bein'
sick all down your good pullover . . . what is it, somethin' to
do with our painting'?
(*A faint snore.*)
Ho, I'm talkin' to you! Is it somethin' to do with our
paintin', I'm askin'?

MACBRYDE: Of course it's to do with our painting', what the fuck
else would it be to do with? What Barker says is if we want to
delve into our Celtic past . . . do it. If we want to pinch from
Picasso . . . do it. If we want an exhibition in Bond Street,
just fuckin' do it!
(*A lengthy pause.*)

COLQUHOUN: And?

MACBRYDE: And what? That's it.

COLQUHOUN: That's the 'Great Idea'?

MACBRYDE: In essence, aye.

COLQUHOUN: That's what took you and Barker *fourteen hours* at this Colony Club to come up with?

MACBRYDE: No, we moved on to the French Pub after about *nine* hours . . .

COLQUHOUN: While I'm sittin' here twiddlin' ma fuckin' thumbs an' starin' at a blank canvas 'cos we havenae enough dough to get ourselves some paint?

MACBRYDE: I wish you wouldnae shout, Rab, you sound exactly like ma Maw.

COLQUHOUN: I wish to Christ I *was* your stupit Maw, I could've strangled you at birth, ya moron!

ALDER: (*From below*) Vozza matter viz you boys, you are shoutink und bawlink so loud? I am not hearink my ears! Zere is some big tragedy I don't know about . . . vot?

MACBRYDE: You havenae got a Thermos you could lend us, have you?

ALDER:(from below) 'Termos'? Wot's zis 'Termos'?

MACBRYDE: (*Impatiently*) For keepin' your tea hot . . . have you got one or have you not got one? A simple yes or no will suffice, or is the whole issue too complex for you?

COLQUHOUN: Don't talk to Jankel like that, he's got a wife and family stranded behind German lines . . .
(*Loudly*) . . . well? Have you got one or have you not got one?
(*To* MACBRYDE) I know I shouldnae be askin', but what the hell do we want a Thermos for?
(*Lights out.*)

Lights up on Bond Street and Lefevre Gallery. Enter COLQUHOUN *and* MACBRYDE *laden with blankets, kettles, Thermos flasks, primus stove, etc.* MACBRYDE *is carrying a hand-painted placard mounted on a pole. They dump blankets etc. outside Gallery.*

COLQUHOUN: So what made you pick the Lefevre Gallery?

MACBRYDE: It's run by a Mr *MacDonald* . . . here, hold this.
(*Hands placard to* COLQUHOUN, *spreads blankets out on pavement. The placard reads: 'We Demand The Same Basic*

Rights As Our ENGLISH Brothers'. COLQUHOUN *stares at it balefully.*)

COLQUHOUN: Which are?

MACBRYDE: Wall space, a weekly wage, an' one or two extras for waitin' out the best part of the War before gettin' wurselves a bloody exhibition . . . I'd get some shuteye if I was you. If we don't get any joy after ten days I'm for packin' it in an' hightailin' it back to Maybole.

COLQUHOUN: Ten days?

MACBRYDE: (*Setting down on 'bed'*) Awright, make it six . . . if this bugger MacDonald hasnae cracked by Day Six Colquhoun an' MacBryde's kaput . . . you'll find some dried eggs in that Thermos for the morn's breakfast . . . you just top it up with hot water from the primus . . . 'night, Rab.

COLQUHOUN: S'that all you've got to say . . . ''night, Rab'?

MACBRYDE: (*Peeking over blanket*) Aw, aye . . . don't stay up too late, you know what a fuckin' crosspatch you are if you don't get your forty winks . . . 'night, Robert.

COLQUHOUN: (*Turning away*) Sufferin' God . . .
(*Lights slowly down.*)

END OF ACT ONE

ACT TWO

Lights slowly up on COLQUHOUN.

COLQUHOUN: Of course the entire business was a bloody farce . . . the dried eggs ran out on Day Two, Day Three saw us frozen to the flagstones . . . by Day Four neither of us could talk we were that hungry . . . Day Six came and went and Mr MacDonald our saviour 'elect' still hadnae put in an appearance, so on the Seventh Day me and Bobby tossed our last remainin' ha'penny to decide what one of us should beg the next passing Army officer to shoot us where we sat . . . by Day Eight, however, the tide began to turn . . . we even got ourselves on to 'Radio Newsreel' . . . parallels were drawn with Gandhi's 'non-violent fasts', then just as swiftly *with*drawn when MacBryde skelped the interviewer's ear after denying him a bite of her sausage roll . . . Then as the morning of Day Twelve approached . . . a miracle!

(*Lights up on galaxy of Colquhoun and MacBryde paintings at Lefevre Gallery. Enter* MACBRYDE *in kilt. Pops champagne cork, pours two glasses.*)

MACBRYDE: Here's tae us, wha's like us? If it hadnae been for my ingenuity, tenacity, an' secondhand Thermos you an' I might've been thumbin' a lift back up to Sconnie Botland to face the scorn of our old Art School alumni, all of whom were either too feart or too feeble to grasp the nettle an' run with it.

COLQUHOUN: (*Raising glass*) Colquhoun and MacBryde!

MACBRYDE: MacBryde an' Colquhoun!

(*They chink glasses, drain them. Refill them. Enter* ADLER.)

ADLER: I hate to be ze bearer of good tidingks but you just sold a picture.

MACBRYDE: D'you hear that, Robert? We just sold a picture!

COLQUHOUN: Eeeeeha!

MACBRYDE: Eeeeeha!

COLQUHOUN/MACBRYDE: (*Together*) Eeeeeeeeeeeeeha!

ADLER: I vould go easy on ze sauce, youse two, remember ze old sayingk . . . 'if vun svallow does not a summer make nor bars ze nightingale.'

34

MACBRYDE: Aye, fine . . . why don't you bugger off, Jankel . . . take your mordant East European wit an' depress some other poor bastards with it . . . (*Raising his glass*) . . . Colquhoun an' MacBryde!

COLQUHOUN: (*Sings*)
     Cauld winter was howlin'
     O'er moor and o'er mountain . . .

COLQUHOUN/MACBRYDE: (*Sing*)
     . . . And dark was the sky
     O'er the deep rolling sea (*etc.*)

ADLER: (*Over singing*) Look at youse, you'd zink it was *shortbreid* you was sellingk . . . paintingk is a serious business!
     (COLQUHOUN *and* MACBRYDE *stop singing, stare at* ADLER.)

ADLER: (*Quietly*) Paintingk is a serious endeavour, not a fucking variety show. Next zingk ve know you vant your name up in light-bulbs!
     (*Turns on his heel, strides off. Pause.*)

COLQUHOUN: (*Soberly*) He might have a point there, Robert . . . I mean it's not exactly dignified for us to behave like a couple of hooligans instead of the sober and dedicated . . .

MACBRYDE: Ayah, bugger, there goes another one!

COLQUHOUN: (*Eagerly*) Where?

MACBRYDE: And another! Wee guy from the Tate's just glued a red sticker to your big 'Jumpin Cat' paintin'!

COLQUHOUN: Yaaaahoo!
     (*Lights snap out. Pause.*)
     (*From blackout*) I was tired.

MACBRYDE: (*From blackout*) You were drunk.

COLQUHOUN: (*From blackout*) I was tired, dammit!

Light slowly up.

MACBRYDE: You were *drunk*, Robert.
     (*A restaurant in Soho.* COLQUHOUN *and* MACBRYDE *seated at table, both wearing dark glasses. A* WAITER *hovers in the background.*)

COLQUHOUN: Awright, so I was drunk, so what? If a chap cannae get drunk at his own Private View where can he get drunk?

MACBRYDE: You werenae just drunk, Rab, you were

disgustingly, nauseatingly, *obscenely* drunk . . . I had to carry
you up six flights of stairs when we got back an' it wasnae
your Private View, it was our Private View.

(*Pause.*)

Six flights, Robert.

COLQUHOUN: Heavy, was I?

MACBRYDE: How would I know? I was *paralettic*. Some Private
View, eh?

(*Loudly, to* WAITER) You wouldnae happen to have a menus
in Braille, would you?

(WAITER *crosses.*)

COLQUHOUN: Aw, God . . . it's just comin' back to me . . . please
say it wasnae me that was violently sick all over the critic
from the *Daily Telegraph*.

MACBRYDE: It wasnae you that was violently sick all over the
critic from the *Daily Telegraph*.

(*Takes menus from* WAITER.)

COLQUHOUN: Thank Christ for that.

MACBRYDE: It was me . . . *you* were violently sick all over the
critic from the *Observer*.

COLQUHOUN: Stop, stop, I cannae take any more.

MACBRYDE: (*Consulting his menu*) What would you like to drink
with your grub? There's a twelve an' six claret here for two
an' eleven.

COLQUHOUN: Don't . . . I couldnae look at another drink an' it
should be somethin' white, claret doesnae go with snook.

WAITER: Are we ready to order, gentlemen?

MACBRYDE: The grub, no, the gargles, yes . . . we'll have a
magnum of your finest champagne substitute for openers.

COLQUHOUN: I told you, I don't want anythin' to drink.

WAITER: Perhaps the gentleman would care to choose from our
wide range of fruit cordials? I've just presented a very
acceptable pear and parsnip 'potage' to some *uniformed*
diners in the alcove yonder.

(COLQUHOUN *cranes round to see where the 'uniformed diners'
are seated.*)

MACBRYDE: This gentleman happens to be Scottish, my good
fellow, it's against his religion to touch anything non-

36

alcoholic, he'll have what the rest of us are drinkin'.

WAITER: Very good, sir.

(*Glides off.*)

MACBRYDE: Wee drop of champagne from Kuala Lumpur, Rab, take the edge off your hangover.

COLQUHOUN: It isnae just the hangover, I'm depressed.

MACBRYDE: What you '*depressed*' about? We've just had our first Bond Street exhibition, stuff's sellin' like hot cakes, we'll get reviewed in the nationals, the brightest of futures is bein' forecast . . . what about the poor bastards in the trenches, up to here in shite an' shrapnel? Now, if one of them told me he was 'depressed', that I could accept . . . Christ, there but for a dose of junior tuberculosis an' a dickey ticker go you an' I, old son.

COLQUHOUN: That's what I'm depressed about, ya mug.

MACBRYDE: Well, don't be . . . accordin' to the wireless the dugouts in the desert are in a worse state than the outside toilets at Seventy-seven Bedford Gardens . . .

(*To unseen military personnel*) . . . aye, we know it isnae exactly a *picnic* across there but nor is it all 'cakes an' ale' back here on the Home Front . . . we're havin' to paint with *coconut* oil instead of linseed . . . DRIVE YOU NUTS.

(*To* COLQUHOUN) . . . these buggers've got it cushy, you know . . . free smokes, free meals, free uniforms . . . we should *all* be that lucky.

(WAITER *arrives with champagne and ice bucket. He is wearing Army forage cap. Sets ice bucket down. Withdraws.*)

COLQUHOUN: I know he doesnae know it yet, but what is friend Barker treatin' us to champagne for?

MACBRYDE: Guilt, Rab. Like your good self he is consumed by an overwhelming sense of guilt, but with greater justification . . . d'you not remember him arrivin' at the fag end of the Private View an' regalin' all and sundry with news about his 'commission'?

COLQUHOUN: No, I don't.

MACBRYDE: Of course, everybody naturally assumed he meant a 'commission' in H.M. Forces, started slappin' him on the back an' tellin' him what a 'brave chap' he was . . .

COLQUHOUN: But?

MACBRYDE: . . . turns out it's a 'commission' for some poetry anthology, has to beetle off to America, hence the invite for eats . . . doesnae want you an' I to think he's a 'deserter', does he?

(WAITER *reappears wearing Army tunic in addition to forage cap. Starts uncorking champagne.*)

(*To* WAITER) Aye, very subtle . . . what about us poor mugs left behind to face the bombs an' the blackout an' the absence of bon-bons?

WAITER: I didn't say a thing, sir.

MACBRYDE: (*To* COLQUHOUN) Cheeky bastard.

(COLQUHOUN *clutches his head and groans. Enter* BARKER.)

BARKER: (*Slinging gas-mask haversack over chairback*) Bloody good review in the *Telegraph* . . .

MACBRYDE: You hear that, Robert?

BARKER: . . . what's up with him?

MACBRYDE: Nothin' a cup of bubbly cannae cure. How good?

BARKER: (*Unfolding* Daily Telegraph) Too bloody good, if you ask me . . . build you up to beat the shit out of you later . . . trust me, I ought to know . . . (*Passing newspaper to* MACBRYDE) . . . what're we having?

MACBRYDE: (*Leafing through newspaper*) The snook comes 'highly recommended' . . . with the stress on highly . . . what page we on?

WAITER: (*Pouring 'champagne'*) We do have some poultry just arrived, gentlemen.

MACBRYDE: Nice wee bit of chicken, Robert, 'cock a *snook*' at the rest of the world, no?

BARKER: Page five.

MACBRYDE: (*To waiter*) Three snook, pal.

BARKER: No, hang on, make that two, I'll have the Corned Beef Wellington.

WAITER: A wise choice, if I may say so, sir.

BARKER: (*To* MACBRYDE *reading review*) Describes you as a pair of 'Celtic lyricists', you could sue the buggers.

(*Takes sip of champagne substitute.* WAITER *withdraws.*)

Fucking Norah . . .

MACBRYDE: Ho, pin back your lugs, Robert . . . (*Reads*)
'Impressive Debut At Reid and Lefevre . . . Two young
Scots, one of them a "figurist" in the Modern manner, the
other a still-life painter of some distinction . . .'

COLQUHOUN: (*Overlapping*) Sick, sick, sick, sick . . . I know I
should feel elated but I don't . . . I feel sick to my bloody
stomach . . . the Angel of Death hovering in the wings, the
rest of Europe a Theatre of war, us here, centre-stage,
oblivious to the charnel house that's France, Poland, Italy,
slugging champagne and salivatin' over mentions in the
bloody papers!
(*Sweeps his full glass of champagne on to floor.*)

BARKER: Wise move, old chap, tastes like armadillo piss.
(*To* MACBRYDE) Why is our waiter dressed up in Army
cast-offs?
(WAITER *reappears. He is now completely rigged out in khaki.*)

WAITER: 'Vegetable of the Day' is carrot, gentlemen.

BARKER: Oh, fuck . . .
(*Clamps a hand over his mouth.*)

MACBRYDE: Yes, lashings of carrots, my man . . . what's good
enough for our gallant airmen is good enough for me . . .
when was the last time you saw a bunny wearing goggles?
Allow me to top you up, Robert.
(*Refills another glass for* COLQUHOUN.)

COLQUHOUN: Sick . . . we're all sick . . .

WAITER: (*To* MACBRYDE) If the gentleman's feeling unwell, sir, I
shouldn't recommend any more champagne in the
meantime.

MACBRYDE: The gentleman's feeling absolutely hunky-dory,
aren't you, Robert? C'mon, give us one of your big sunny
smiles, this's supposed to be a celebration, for Christ's sake.

COLQUHOUN: 'Celebration'? What're we *celebratin'*, our
combined talents for dodgin' the column!
(*Gets to his feet, rocks table.*)

BARKER: (*Recovering*) Steady on, old chap, if that remark's aimed
at me . . .

COLQUHOUN: You know what they say, Georgie Boy . . . if the
cap fits . . .

(*Plucks forage cap from* WAITER'*s head, crams it on to*
BARKER'*s and pulls it down over his eyes.*)
. . . this country's about to go under, the least you could do is
stay behind and man the barricades like the rest of us!

BARKER: (*Getting to his feet*) I'm not going to sit here and . . .

COLQUHOUN: You're not goin' anywhere, ya fucker!
(*Grabs* BARKER *by lapels.*)

BARKER: Aaaargh!

WAITER: I'll just fetch your lunch, gentlemen.
(*Exits.*)

COLQUHOUN: What is it Winnie says in your precious *Telegraph*
. . . 'Give us the tools . . .'? It's us that're the 'tools' . . .
useless bloody tools that're only good at screwin' themselves
an' each other!

BARKER: How dare you? I am a raving heterosexual!

MACBRYDE: Oh, look, Robert . . . here's your snook.
(WAITER *breezes back on with trolley.*)

BARKER: (*To* COLQUHOUN) Fuck off!

WAITER: (*To* MACBRYDE) Snook, sir?
(BARKER *manages to break* COLQUHOUN'*s grip, sits down with
a thump, wrenches at forage cap pulled over his eyes.*)

WAITER: Corned Beef Wellington?

BARKER: Yes!

MACBRYDE: (*Leaning across to* COLQUHOUN) I think we should
have a wee nap when we get back to Bedford Gardens . . .
(COLQUHOUN *throws back his head and howls.* WAITER *waits
until howling subsides and* COLQUHOUN'*s head drops on to
table.*)

WAITER: (*To* MACBRYDE) What would you like done with the
gentleman's snook, sir?
(*Lights down.*)

*A flash lights up the stage for a second. Then another. Lights up on
Soho Square, where* PHOTOGRAPHER *is setting up his Gondolfi.
Enter* JOURNALIST *in belted trenchcoat. He glances at his watch.*

PHOTOGRAPHER: Used to knock about with a couple of Scotch
queers in Lambeth. Little 'un was a redhead . . . 'exotic'
dancer . . . double-jointed . . . name of 'Shirley' . . . big chap

was Merchant Navy . . . chronic alcoholic . . . nice enough to talk to but when you think what they must've got up to, makes your hair stand on end, dunnit . . . I got nothing against 'em, meself . . . live and let live, I say, but what' they ought to do is introduce some barbed wire up their jaxies, give the buggers a fright.

(*Enter* COLQUHOUN *and* MACBRYDE. MACBRYDE'*s eyes are screwed shut. They both look unwell.*)

COLQUHOUN: Springtime in Soho . . . a Lark in the Park with the *Picture Post* . . . Colquhoun and MacBryde are the Toast of the Town, I wish I felt better, I wish I was drunk.

(*They take up their position in front of the camera.*)

MACBRYDE: You didnae happen to catch sight of the mischievous elf that stitched my eyelids together durin' the night, did you?

COLQUHOUN: Smile, Robert.

(*A flash as* PHOTOGRAPHER *takes photo.*)

MACBRYDE: (*Recoiling*) Ahyah, bastard.

JOURNALIST: Tell me, Mr Colquhoun, what d'you make of Wyndham Lewis describing you as the 'best young English painter of his generation', were you slightly over-awed by that?

MACBRYDE: Most certainly not . . . Lewis only got it half right. This man is a *genius*. Not only is he the best young painter of his *own* generation but Wyndham bloody Lewis's *and* every other generation back to and including Hogarth's . . . and for your information he is not . . . repeat *not* . . . English . . . nor, come to that, am I . . . we are both Internationalists.

(*Another flash.*)

COLQUHOUN: We recognize no frontiers.

MACBRYDE: Carry no passports.

COLQUHOUN: Our only Identity Cards are those you find hanging on the walls at Reid and Lefevre.

MACBRYDE: We belong to the Brotherhood of Artists, all of us speaking the same language . . .

COLQUHOUN: . . . some more fluently than others, it must be said.

MACBRYDE: Talk is cheap, true Art is beyond price.

(*Another flash.*)

JOURNALIST: I believe your current exhibition has done very well, a number of pictures going for as much as two hundred pounds . . . What's your reaction to such enormous prices, given that most people in Britain are having to make do on next to . . .

COLQUHOUN: (*Overlapping*) Yes, we do realize there's a War on and, yes, we are making a substantial donation to the Red Cross . . .

MACBRYDE: (*Sharply*) What?

COLQUHOUN: . . . now, if that's the interview over we'd like to . . .

JOURNALIST: I'm sure I've read somewhere that one of you was a 'conscientious objector', is that correct?

MACBRYDE: You print anythin' like that in your periodical an' I'll personally put your lamps out, pal.

PHOTOGRAPHER: Hold it.

(*Another flash.*)

MACBRYDE: This man was practically Monty's batman prior to the illness that forced him to cut short his six weeks' Basic Training and return to Civvy Street and his God-given role as our Greatest Living Artist . . . Colquhoun a 'conshie'? How dare you! Smile, Robert.

(*Another flash.*)

JOURNALIST: Fine, just thought I'd clear that up . . .

COLQUHOUN: I've got angina.

MACBRYDE: He's got nothin' of the kind . . .

(*To* COLQUHOUN) . . . what you tellin' him that for? I'll fuckin' murder you!

JOURNALIST: . . . Let me read you a quote . . . (*Leafs through notebook. Reads.*) '. . . it is wrong for us to think of them as a couple, rather as a single organism, so closely bound are they in striving towards a coherent pictorial language . . .'

PHOTOGRAPHER: Bit closer together, I'm losing you either side of frame . . .

(*Another flash.*)

JOURNALIST: '. . . a language that sometimes borrows certain phrases, indeed, at other times, whole passages from Picasso,

and yet contrives, by what mysterious means it is impossible
to analyse, to retain its own native integrity . . .'

JOURNALIST/COLQUHOUN/MACBRYDE: (*Together*) '. . . rooted as
it is in the ancient bedrock of their combined Celtic past.'

MACBRYDE: Well, that's a new one on me . . .

COLQUHOUN: Bloody liar.

JOURNALIST: (*To* COLQUHOUN) Would you care to comment?

COLQUHOUN: Aye, just give me a second . . . whilst confessing to
a certain frisson at the prospect of our phissogs gettin'
plastered all over the pages of the *Picture Post*, I have a
nagging suspicion that this particular paragraph, lifted as it
was from the 'Letters' column of the *Kilmarnock Advertiser*
and reprinted without permission in the latest issue of *Art
News & Review*, could, were it run alongside our grotesquely
enlarged features in the popular weekly, prove to be the
petard by which we are hoist . . .
(*To* JOURNALIST) . . . I think I'm right in saying it was
originally signed 'An Art Lover, Maybole'?

JOURNALIST: Pardon me?

MACBRYDE: (*To* COLQUHOUN) What you lookin' at us like that
for?

PHOTOGRAPHER: Last one . . . steady.
(*Another flash.*)

JOURNALIST: Thank you very much.

MACBRYDE: C'mon, we've just got time to sink a coupla pints
before we meet up with this dunce from the *Daily Mail* for
drinks. (*Takes* COLQUHOUN's *arm.*)
(*To* JOURNALIST) Thanks, gents.
(*Steers* COLQUHOUN *towards exit.*) We're creatin' our own
legends, Rab . . . we're creatin' our own legends!

COLQUHOUN: (*Looking back over his shoulder*) Aye, I'm afraid you
might be right, Bobby son.
(*Exeunt.*)

PHOTOGRAPHER: Right, where to next, my son? (*Consults notes*) I
got 'Jellied Eels' down here but I don't recall if that's a
'feature' or what I got to fetch back . . . we got the wife's
mum coming up from the East End . . . 'orrible woman.
'You still taking them snaps for what's-name? Why don't he

get himself a proper job, Edith, like what your dad's got?'
Edith's dad's got a fruitstall down the market . . . pot-bellied
geezer with one leg . . . drinks like a fish . . . d'you think
them two was drunk? The Scotch gits?
(*Lights down.*)

Sound of toilet flushing.
MACBRYDE: (*In blackout*) Are you nearly ready, Rab?
(*Lights up on Bedford Gardens.*)
(*Enter* MACBRYDE, *no longer in kilt but doing up pair of baggy
denim trousers. He bends, lifts rug, discovers similar pair of
denim trousers underneath, picks them up, examines them. They
are pretty crumpled. He replaces them under rug, walks back and
forth on top of it to press trousers underneath.*)
C'mon, we'll need to get a move on.
(COLQUHOUN *appears from behind scullery screen in shirt tail,
face covered in shaving lather.*)
COLQUHOUN: Chuck nagging us, I cannae find that razor blade.
MACBRYDE: You're an artist, you're growin' a beard. Hurry up,
these dungarees feel about ready.
COLQUHOUN: How many times d'you have to be told, they are
not dungarees, they're denim troosers . . . I bought a 'Seven
O'Clock' blade this mornin', it cannae just've vanished.
MACBRYDE: It didnae. I had to cut a big chunk off the leg of these
dung . . . sorry . . . these denim troosers.
COLQUHOUN: Aw, that's brilliant. You're meant to roll them up
. . . you never seen any 'Bowery Boys' movies?
MACBRYDE: Nup . . . what are they, dressmakin' pitchers?
ADLER: (*Off*) Hullo? You zere?
(COLQUHOUN *dodges back behind screen.*)
MACBRYDE: (*Loudly*) It's open.
(*Enter* ADLER. *He is carrying a newspaper. He looks stunned.*)
ADLER: You seen zis? General Sikorski's been killed.
MACBRYDE: Aye, very nice . . . (*Loudly*) . . . that's Jankel, d'you
want to invite him to the exhibition?
(*To* ADLER) He's havin' a show of monotypes at Lefevre,
d'you want to tag along for the jaunt? Starts at seven.
ADLER: Of course, zey murder him . . . after zey find all zese

44

officers at Katyn Forest . . . dead . . . slaughtered . . . ze Allied
Zecret Zervice fucking murder ze vun man that believes ze
Chermans ven zey say it is ze Russians . . .
(MACBRYDE *peels back rug, picks up crumpled denims, holds
them up for inspection.* ADLER *buries face in newspaper.*)

MACBRYDE: Robert? Sorry, Jankel, very important exhibition . . .
consolidate . . . follow up . . . cannae rest on our laurels, who
was it you said got killed?

ADLER: . . . fucking Vinnie . . . fucking Vinston Churchill . . .
(COLQUHOUN's *head appears round scullery screen, scraps of
newspaper stuck to his face where he's cut himself.*)

COLQUHOUN: Winston Churchill?

MACBRYDE: That's what happens to Sunday painters, Robert. (*To*
ADLER) Whodunnit, the Euston Road mob? Here . . . catch.
(*Chucks crumpled denims to* COLQUHOUN *who fails to take any
notice. They fall on floor.*)

ADLER: No, no, I mean, Vinston Churchill is at ze back of it.

COLQUHOUN: (*To* MACBRYDE) At the back of what? What's he
talkin' about?

MACBRYDE: Haven't the foggiest . . . you realize we'll have to get a
taxi now?

ADLER: Vy you vearingk dungarees, you working in factory
nightshift, vot?

MACBRYDE: (*Hunting around for taxi money*) They arenae
dungarees, they're denim troosers . . .

COLQUHOUN: (*Bending to pick up crumpled denims*) Bloody hell . . .

MACBRYDE: . . . George Barker sent them from the States . . . all
your big American artists are wearin' them . . . the beauty, of
course, being that once the arse is out of them all you have to
do is cut up what's left, nail it to some stretchers, an' 'Hey,
presto', your next canvas. (*Discovering pair of spectacles*)
Hullo, what's this?

COLQUHOUN: (*Denims half-on, half-off*) I cannae put these on . . .
(*Spotting* MACBRYDE *with specs*) . . . hoi, watch what you're
doin' with them, I've only just . . .

MACBRYDE: Artists don't wear specs. (*Drops them, crushes them
underfoot.*)

COLQUHOUN: Ya bloody . . .! Did you see that, Jankel?

ADLER: (*Putting own specs on*) See vot?

MACBRYDE: (*Crossing*) I found two half-dollars, c'mon, get them dungarees on, you cannae expect the bourgeoisie to fork out for a Colquhoun original if I'm not there at their elbows letting' them know what a wise investment they've made. (COLQUHOUN *crosses, picks up broken specs, sticks them on, peers down at crumpled denims.*)

COLQUHOUN: Christ's sake, they're even worse lookin' through these, could you not've pressed them for us?

MACBRYDE: I did press them . . . gimme those . . . (*Plucks specs from* COLQUHOUN'*s nose.*) . . . you get spotted in goggles an' them monotypes of yours arenae worth the paper they're printed on. Tell him, Jankel.

ADLER: (*Looking up from paper*) Tell him vot . . . about Sikorski? I already tell you both, you don't give a shit, all you care about is your stoopid denim dungarees and your stoopid fucking monotypes . . . I tell you somethingk else, I hope your stoopid taxi crash, you both get dead, then you know vot happen Sikorski . . . I go, I don't come back . . . you vanna talk with me, stick your arse oot ze vindy.
(*Stomps out.* COLQUHOUN *and* MACBRYDE *look at each other.*)

MACBRYDE: What the fuck's eatin' him?

COLQUHOUN: Well, whatever it is it cannae be anywhere as bad as what's eatin' me . . . look at the state of these dungarees!

Lights up on Embankment. COLQUHOUN *enters and sits on bench, opens copy of* Picture Post. *Bombs falling in middle distance.*

COLQUHOUN: (*Reads*) '. . . it is wrong, or at least misguided, to consider them as a couple . . . they are better described as a single organism . . . The Best Thing To Have Happened To British Art Since Winnie Shut The Lid On His Paintbox and Concentrated On Putting Adolf "On The Canvas".' (*Looks up.*) Not quite how Herbert Read might've put it but still . . . (*Enter* MACBRYDE *with two coffee mugs.*)

MACBRYDE: I was goin' to get you a pie but they didnae have any . . . here.
(*Hands mug to* COLQUHOUN. *Takes out hip flask.*)
Happy?

COLQUHOUN: Very. I came across a toenail in that last one you
     bought me.
     (MACBRYDE, *about to top up mugs from hip flask, stops.*)
     Aye, aye, I'm happy, I'm happy.
     (MACBRYDE *tops mugs up.*)
MACBRYDE: We've done it, Rab . . . I mean, we've really done it!
     There must be half a million jokers buy the *Picture Post*, give
     us another gander . . .
     (*Takes* Picture Post *from* COLQUHOUN, *spreads it out on
     bench.*)
     Know somethin'? I actually look quite distinguished . . .
     apart from the snotters on ma jersey . . . don't you think?
     Well, I think I do . . . there was a wumman at your
     exhibition the night that came up to me an' said 'Mr
     MacBryde? Lady Cosgrove . . . my companions and I think
     you are the handsomest man in the whole of London . . . tell
     me, are you "spoken for"?'
COLQUHOUN: How marvellously quaint . . .
MACBRYDE: To which I replied . . . 'Your Ladyship, not only am
     I "spoken for" but I am walking out with . . . nay, let us not
     beat about the bush . . . I am *shagging* the gorgeous Mr
     Colquhoun yonder . . . the love of my life and the Best
     Dressed Man In England . . . look at the way his denim
     troosers hing.'
COLQUHOUN: (*Looking down*) I quite like them crumpled . . .
     You know how I went out this mornin' . . .
     (*Looks up.*)
MACBRYDE: To get some turps, aye . . .?
COLQUHOUN: I went to Gower Street.
MACBRYDE: For turps?
COLQUHOUN: To sign up . . . as an ambulance driver. I report
     tomorrow night at seven o'clock sharp.
MACBRYDE: You cannae drive, Rab.
COLQUHOUN: I know.
MACBRYDE: They didnae see that as a drawback, no?
COLQUHOUN: I just didnae tell them . . . said to the guy I'd been
     invalided out the Army and I wanted very much to be of
     some use, guy said 'Sign here', so I did . . . gave us a pair of

gauntlets and an armband with 'Ambulance Driver' on it . . .
hadnae the heart to tell him.

MACBRYDE: Wish I hadnae smashed your specs now . . . nothin'
worse than a short-sighted ambulance driver that cannae
drive an ambulance . . . your monotypes look beautiful, by
the way.

COLQUHOUN: You're not angry, then?

MACBRYDE: I'm very proud.

COLQUHOUN: About the monotypes or me volunteerin'?

MACBRYDE: C'mere.

(*He puts an arm round* COLQUHOUN's *neck, draws him close.
Lights down.*)

*Sound of heavy bombing, air raid sirens, general chaos of the Blitz.
Lights up on French Pub interior.* COLQUHOUN *wearing Auxiliary
Ambulance Service armband.*

COLQUHOUN: Well, this's it . . . one more quarter gill, a quick
shufti at the Highway Code, then it's out into the Jaws of
Hell . . .
Jesus. Didnae imagine I was goin' to be this shaky . . . still,
it's some kinda balm . . . no more nightmares . . . no more
walkin' down the street starin' at the pavement . . .
(*Checks overcoat pockets.*) . . . got my sketchbook, got my
inks . . . don't want the embarrassment of bumpin' into
Henry Moore down the tube station without the tools of my
trade on us . . .
(*Puts driver's hat on.*) . . . 'mirror . . . signal . . . manouevre.
Mirror . . . signal . . . manouevre . . .'
(*Enter* MACBRYDE. *He is dressed in the kilt.*)

MACBRYDE: Just spotted the traveller from Bell's dumpin' a
half-crate of whisky down their delivery chute.

COLQUHOUN: Back in the full regalia, you'll notice, though
strangely enough, he's been behaving himself of late . . . only
seven walk-outs at last night's Private View . . . I better shoot
off, Bobby . . . (*Dons driving gauntlets.*) . . . Listen, don't
overdo it, d'you hear me?

MACBRYDE: 'Overdo it'? When've you ever known me to 'overdo
it', Rab?

48

(*Turning to bar at large*) Right, this's your last chance . . . any you lot of limp-wristed *English* artists fancy a dram . . . no? None of you imitation Kit Woods or ersatz Henry Tonkses care for a wee 'deoch an' doris' afore my sweetheart here has tae gang awa'? Tell them where you're gangin' awa' tae, Robert . . . on you go, tell the buggers . . . you see this man here? This's Robert Colquhoun . . . that's right, Robert Colquhoun . . . you'll find me an' Robert gracing the current pages of *Picture Post* alongside my good self . . . hands up who's seen it?

COLQUHOUN: Right, I'm off . . . don't do anythin' daft, are you listenin'? Behave, right?

(*Heads for exit.*)

MACBRYDE: Come back here, ya bugger, where d'you think you're goin'?

COLQUHOUN: (*To barman*) If he gets too outrageous put a call through to Gower Street, we'll send an ambulance.

MACBRYDE: Robert?

COLQUHOUN: Wish me luck.

(*Exits.*)

MACBRYDE: Rab? Get you back here . . . Rab!

(BARMAN *places two large whiskies on counter.*)

BARMAN: You will keep it down, sir?

MACBRYDE: 'Course I'll keep it down, the only thing I ever threw up was the chance to be recognized.

(*To bar at large*) You know who that was that just went out, don't you? Out into the flak an' the flyin' bombs at the steerin' wheel of his first ambulance to help pull limbless ex-housewives an' their kiddies from the rubble of their ruined prefabs . . . that's correct . . . Rab Colquhoun . . . the 'best young painter of his generation an' a credit to his country' . . . stand up the man amongst you that can hold a fitch to that fine fellow, there isnae one . . . I've seen your efforts, I've seen your puny daubings . . . you can neither paint nor lea' it alane! (*Has a slug of whisky.*) Aye, an' stand up the man amongst you that has took the King's bawbee, you cannae do that either!

BARMAN: Excuse me . . .

MACBRYDE: You already are excused, barman, you're in a 'reserved occupation', it's this buncha lily-livered tarts *I'm* talkin' to . . . paint? They couldnae paint the camouflage on a coal wagon or the 'dazzle' on a dinghy . . . an' if you're wonderin' why I'm not in khaki it's because I'm seconded to undercover work for H.M. Government . . .
(*Whips round to confront bar at large.*)
. . . Who said 'H.M. Tennant'? Any day now I could be dropped behind enemy lines with nothin' but a Harry Lauder songsheet an' a shoogly walkin' stick, I fail to see anything remotely 'theatrical' about that . . .
(*To* BARMAN) Same again, Sydney. And a round for this collection of nancy boys . . .
(*Rounding on bar at large*) . . . no, I shall not 'Go home, Jock' . . . my heart may be in Maybole but my remaining organs are renting a studio in Notting Hill which I happily share with my darling Robert, to whom I dedicate the following anthem . . .
(*Sings*)
 Just a wee deoch an' doris, just a we yin, that's aw . . .
 Just a wee deoch an' doris afore ye gang awa . . .
 There's a wee wifie waitin' by a wee but an' ben,
 If ye can say it's a braw bricht . . .
C'mon, say it! 'It's a braw bricht moonlicht . . .' *say* it! Let me hear you!
BAR AT LARGE: (*Muted*) '. . . it's a bra' brikt moonlikt nikt . . .'
MACBRYDE: (*Triumphant*) '. . . then you're awricht, ye ken!' And again! 'Just a wee deoch an' doris, just a wee yin, that's aw . . .'
BARMAN: (*To departing regulars*) 'Night, sir . . . 'night, madam . . .
MACBRYDE: '. . . just a wee deoch an' doris afore . . .' (*Cocks an ear.*)
BAR AT LARGE: '. . . ye gang awa' . . .'
MACBRYDE: '. . . there's a wee wifie waitin' . . . sing up!
BAT AT LARGE: '. . . there's a wee wifie waiting . . .'
(*Lights start going down.*)
MACBRYDE: '. . . by a wee but an' ben, an' if ye can say . . .'

BAR AT LARGE: '. . . it's a bra' brikt moonlikt nikt, then you're
    arikt, you ken . . .'
MACBRYDE: And again, ya bastards!
    (*Sings*)
        Just a wee deoch an' doris, just a wee yin, that's aw,
        Just a wee deoch an' doris (*etc.*)
    (*Lights slowly down.*)

Lights up on COLQUHOUN.
COLQUHOUN: You can add to that list the Swiss Pub, the Black
    Horse, the Bricklayers Arms, the Fitzroy, Duke of York,
    and the Marquess of Granby . . . well, I mean, who wants to
    stroll into their local for a 'small refreshment' only to find
    themselves confronted, by MacBryde's bare arse and an
    invitation to 'put a penny in the *slot* to help the War
    Blinded'?
    (Lights up on MACBRYDE *seated on train.* COLQUHOUN *joins
    him.*)
COLQUHOUN: Cannae let you out ma sight for a second, can I?
    There isnae a pub left in Soho that'll serve us an' believe you
    me that takes some doin' . . . give us that postcard.
    (*Snatches picture postcard from* MACBRYDE).
MACBRYDE: Thought he wasnae comin' back till the end of the
    war? I certainly wouldnae . . . what'd you tell the ambulance
    depot?
COLQUHOUN: To phone the Luftwaffe an' ask them to go easy on
    the bombin' over the weekend, what d'you think I told
    them? (*Reading postcard*) He says here that the landlord of
    the local hostelry is 'very obliging'.
    (*Blackout as train goes into tunnel.*)
MACBRYDE: (*In blackout*) Shouts out 'Time, gentlemen, please' in
    the Doric, you mean? Aye, thanks a bunch, Georgie Boy.
COLQUHOUN: (*In blackout*) You don't *have* to come, you know.
MACBRYDE: An' miss aw the carry-on with the kiddies? You must
    be jokin'. (*Pause.*) Wish we could have one, Rab.
COLQUHOUN: One what?
MACBRYDE: A kiddie.
COLQUHOUN: Shuttup.

Lights up on sailing dinghy with MACBRYDE *standing proudly in the prow, hair and kilt flying in the breeze.* COLQUHOUN *sits in the middle,* GEORGE BARKER *at the tiller.* COLQUHOUN *is reading a book. They each have a drink in their fist.*

MACBRYDE: (*Sings*)

>Speed, bonnie boat, like a bird on the wing,
>Over the sea to Skye . . .
>Carry the lad that's born to be king,
>Onward the sailors cry . . . (*etc.*)

COLQUHOUN: (*Glancing up from book*) Still nineteen forty-three . . . Rudolf Hess's parachuted into Scotland, the Allies've landed in Normandy, and Bobby and I have baled out to Barker's 'bolthole' on the Essex marshes . . . (*Turning*) . . . George, you're the skipper, order that noisy bastard below decks before he has the lot of us in the drink.

MACBRYDE: (*Breaks off singing*) Drink? Did I hear somebody mention 'drink'? I don't mind if I do, sir.
(*Chucks his empty tumbler to* BARKER, *who refills it from a bottle of bourbon.*)

BARKER: So, tell me, how's London life? Lizzie reckons you pair are becoming pretty fucking famous these days . . .

MACBRYDE: *Famous* isnae in it, Georgie Boy . . . we're ridin' the crest of a wave, Robert an' I . . . two corks bobbing along on a tide of recognition, charting a new course on the choppy waters of contemporary Art . . . discovering hitherto unexplored islands, unmapped territories, unimagined archipelagos . . . the most celebrated 'tars' aboard the good ship 'Neo-Romanticism' . . . there's even talk of us representin' our homeland at the first post-war Biennale but they're havin' a big problem comin' up with enough kilts in the right kinda tartan to stitch up into a patchwork pavilion . . . (*Sways dramatically, clutches on to mast.*) . . . whoa!

BARKER: (*To* COLQUHOUN) I take it this *is* just a weekend visit, old chap?

COLQUHOUN: He may be a 'Friend of Dorothy's', George, but at this precise moment he ain't no pal of mine . . . soon as we make landfall he's gettin' poured into a taxi . . . why d'you have to go and spoil everythin'?

MACBRYDE: Who . . . me?
(*Lights out.*)

Clack-clack of typewriter in blackout. Lights up on Tilty Mill interior.
BARKER *in dressing gown paces back and forth, deep in thought.*
Laughter and shrieks of unseen children. Typewriter stops. BARKER
stops pacing.
BARKER: What? (*Listens. Crosses to door. Opens it.*) I can't hear
   you . . . what?
   (*Laughter and shrieking of children louder.*)
   (*Loudly*) I still can't bloody well hear you . . . what?
   (*Thundering of many feet on stairs, followed by more screams,*
   laughter, whooping.)
   (*Over din*) No, the first version . . . 'Sat *Me* Down and Wept'
   is completely American and totally fucking illiterate!
   (*To himself*) Stupid cow . . .
   (MACBRYDE *suddenly appears from nowhere, running at*
   breakneck speed, dressed like a Red Indian and whooping at the
   top of his lungs. He circles BARKER *several times before*
   disappearing again in a different direction. As BARKER *watches*
   him go, COLQUHOUN *comes bursting into the room at his back,*
   feathers stuck into home-made headdress and brandishing a
   tomahawk.)
COLQUHOUN: (*Out of breath*) Where'd he go?
   (BARKER *stares at him balefully.*)
   Where did he go!
BARKER: My dear Robert, it goes without saying that you and
   Robert are always most welcome at Tilty Mill but *ten fucking*
   months? A bit steep even by your standards . . .
COLQUHOUN: (*Overlapping*) Waaaaaah!
   (*Takes off like a rocket, pursued by* MACBRYDE. *Much shouting,*
   laughter, squeals. BARKER *puts his head in his hands. Lights*
   slowly down.)

Lights up on local pub. COLQUHOUN *and* MACBRYDE *propping up*
bar. COLQUHOUN *leafing through* Art News & Review.
MACBRYDE: Don't know what you're so down in the bloody
   mouth about, Johnny Minton's a featherweight . . . that

53

must be his *forty-second* exhibition this year an' it's not even bloody March. (*Loudly*) We'll have another coupla big ones, landlord, an' a wee somethin' for your good self . . . stick it on Mr Barker's slate an' keep your thumb out the measure this time.

(*To* COLQUHOUN) Don't know what you're so down in the bloody mouth about, Johnny Minton's a featherweight . . . that must be his *forty-second* exhibition this year an' it's not even . . . (*Breaks off*) . . . very strange echo in here . . . listen, Robert.

(*Listens.*)

COLQUHOUN: Listen, Robert . . .

MACBRYDE: D'you hear it??

COLQUHOUN: . . . stop fuckin' about. It's been nearly a year, for Christ's sake . . . we havenae done a bloody stroke all the time we've been here.

MACBRYDE: Mebbe *you* havenae, I certainly have . . . (*Loudly*) . . . what you wearin' back there, a pair of divin' boots? Get a move on with them whiskies!

(*To* COLQUHOUN) Have a gander at that.

(*Chucks small sketchbook on bartop.* COLQUHOUN *picks it up, starts leafing through it.*)

MACBRYDE: I *was* goin' to show them to Georgie Boy an' Elizabeth the other night . . . mebbe let them have the red chalk drawin' of the wee fulla in his go-chair as a sort of 'thanks for your hospitality' present . . . get the local joiner to knock up a frame for it . . . (*Loudly*) . . . ho! What's keepin' the bloody drink??

(COLQUHOUN *chucks sketchbook onto bartop.*)

Well? You not goin' to say nothin'?

COLQUHOUN: There isnae a lot I *can* say, it's empty.

MACBRYDE: It is not empty, there's at least one drawin' in there that would put Rubens to shame . . . (*Picks up sketchbook, leafs through.*) . . . wee what-d'you-cry-him . . . in his pram . . . where the hell is it? You'll love it, Rab . . . I felt the old butterflies comin' back . . .

COLQUHOUN: (*Banging glass on bartop*) C'mon, ya bastard, hurry up with them refills!

54

(*Lights snap out.*)

COLQUHOUN: (*From blackout*) Aaaaaaaaaaaaaaargh!

BARKER: Bloody hell, what was that? Are you awake, Lizzie?
(*Lights up on* COLQUHOUN, *wild-eyed, tearing at his clothing, on top of smoking bed.*)

COLQUHOUN: Get away from me, ya wee bastards, get away!
(*Flames flicker around his ankles.* BARKER *enters in a rush, dressing gown tails flying.*)

BARKER: What in Christ's name's going on? Lizzie and I are trying to . . .

COLQUHOUN: I am the Phoenix . . . I will arise from the ashes . . .

BARKER: Fucking hell . . .

COLQUHOUN: . . . ashes to ashes, oose to oose . . . butterflies and babies . . .

BARKER: . . . oh, my God, the children. (*Loudly*) Lizzie? Elizabeth!
(*Races out..*)

COLQUHOUN: . . . sprung from the loins of Finn MacCool, born anew at Tilty Mill . . .
(*Enter* MACBRYDE, *half-dressed, half-drunk. He sniffs.*)

MACBRYDE: What've I told you about smokin' in bed, ya stupit bugger?

COLQUHOUN: . . . I am the Phoenix!

MACBRYDE: Jesus Christ! (*Whips kilt off, starts beating at flames.*) I'll give you bloody 'Phoenix', ya irresponsible bastard! When I've got this fire under control you're for a bloody roastin'!

BARKER: (*Off*) Come along, out, out . . . never mind what Uncle Robert's up to, get your things and get out! Elizabeth!

COLQUHOUN: (*Beating at his torso*) Get them away from me . . . get them away!

MACBRYDE: (*Beating at flames*) I told you not to have them pickled eggs . . . (*Loudly*) . . . Barker? Where the hell are you? Barker!

BARKER:(*Off*) What d'you mean, '*your* manuscript'? That's *my* fucking manuscript!

MACBRYDE: Barker, ya bastard!

(BARKER *comes racing in, soda syphon in his hand.*)

BARKER: Don't panic, the books and the children are safe . . . out of my way. (*Shoves* MACBRYDE *to one side.*)

COLQUHOUN: Aaaargh, ma legs're gettin' burnt! The butterflies're goin' to get me . . . help!

BARKER: (*Squirting syphon*) Keep him doused, that's the secret . . .

MACBRYDE: What the hell're you doin'?

BARKER: Don't fret, we've got a spare one downstairs on the drinks trolley . . .

COLQUHOUN: (*To* MACBRYDE) What're you laughin' at?

BARKER:(*Loudly*) What is it now, Lizzie, I'm right in the middle of a fucking crisis! What? (*To* COLQUHOUN) Here, take over, there's a good chap . . . (*Hands syphon to* COLQUHOUN).

(*Loudly*) Alright, alright, I'm on my fucking way! (*Exits hurriedly.*)

(*Off*) Fucking women!

COLQUHOUN: This isnae funny, you! (*Squirts* MACBRYDE *with syphon.*)

MACBRYDE: Ooow, chuck that!

(COLQUHOUN *steps off bed, starts chasing* MACBRYDE *round and round, squirting him with syphon.*)

I'm warnin' you, Robert . . . ohyah!

(*Laughter and chaos. Lights slowly down.*)

Bring up 'Yes, We Have No Bananas' on radio. Lights up on Bedford Gardens. A sense of order and good cheer. MACBRYDE *enters from scullery, sipping from mug of tea and singing along with radio. He crosses to easel, where a small still-life painting is set up. Puts mug down, picks up brushes, does some more to picture, steps back . . . smiles.*

Enter COLQUHOUN, *dripping wet, from street.*

COLQUHOUN: Bedford Gardens, nineteen forty-five . . . London's bombed to buggery but it's better being back than bummin' off Barker . . . (*Removes wet coat, slings it on floor.*) 'fraid Bobby and I ran up a bit of a slate down there . . . twelve hundred and forty-nine pounds, fourteen and six . . . we let

56

him have the fourteen and six and wrote out an I.O.U. for the rest . . . promised to make up the shortfall out of our next exhibition at Lefevre . . . Jesus.

MACBRYDE: Didnae hear you comin' in, Robert . . . well?

COLQUHOUN: Aaahchoo! I think I've caught a chill.

MACBRYDE: You did go and have a blether with MacDonald, I take it?

COLQUHOUN: Look at these shoes, they're absolutely soakin'. (*Starts removing shoes and stuffing them with newspapers.*)

MACBRYDE: Don't ask me how, Rab, but I get the distinct feelin' there's somethin' you're not tellin' me. He wants to up the Gallery's percentage, is that it?

COLQUHOUN: Who does?

MACBRYDE: MacDonald . . . he wants to split the cost of the framin' with you an' me havin' to stump up the lion's share, is that what it is?

COLQUHOUN: (*Examining shoes*) Give us a shout the next time you're passin' a cobblershop, will you?

MACBRYDE: Wait a minute, wait a minute, it's somethin' to do with our 'comeback' exhibition, right?

COLQUHOUN: You're gettin' warm . . . aachoo! Listen, Bobby . . .

MACBRYDE: No, you listen, I'm not upset . . . in fact, I was preparin' maself for it . . . if MacDonald, in his infinite wisdom . . . no, let me finish, Robert . . . if MacDonald wants to have a Colquhoun *solo* exhibition this time around then who am I to stand in your way?

COLQUHOUN: Before you go any further there's somethin' I think I should tell you . . .

MACBRYDE: (*Overlapping*) You see? That was easy, wasn't it? No more Colquhoun an' *MacBryde* at Reid an' Lefevre, just fuckin' Colquhoun, that's fine, I should crawl off under a stone an' die . . . no, don't touch me! Don't try an' comfort me, haven't I always said that *you* were the genius? I've always said that, *even* to bloody Lefevre an' look where it's got me . . . MacDonald goes an' fuckin' drops me! Aye, bloody terrific. I never trusted that bastard . . . I'm not just sayin' that, his eyes're too close thegither *and* he's got a bloody speech impediment . . . he sounds like a fuckin' *Englishman*!

COLQUHOUN: MacDonald's dead, Bobby.

MACBRYDE: Good! I'm delighted!

COLQUHOUN: And it isnae just you they're droppin', it's the both of us.

MACBRYDE: When I think what we've done for that . . . what?

COLQUHOUN: We no longer have any connection with the Lefevre Gallery.

MACBRYDE: What d'you mean, 'No longer any connection'? It was you an' me that put that mausoleum on the map . . . no longer any connection? Before 'Colquhoun an' MacBryde' came along it was a shrine to mediocrity, that joint . . . an elephants' boneyard festooned with 'fine pictures' from the frail and incontinent wankers of Cheyne Walk an' their acolytes . . . did you tell them that, I bet you never!

(Paces to and fro in blind fury.) 'No longer any connection'? 'No longer any *connection*'!

(Stops.) Who was it you said had died . . . MacDonald?

COLQUHOUN: Last Monday, from cancer.

MACBRYDE: Shite.

(Slumps down on bed.)

Did you try the Redfern?

COLQUHOUN: Redfern, Tooth's, Gimpel Fils, Grabowski . . . no dice.

MACBRYDE: There must be somebody interested . . .

COLQUHOUN: There isnae.

MACBRYDE: But we're paintin' better than ever, Rab . . . look at that still life . . . look at the lemon, look at the fuckin' lemon . . . that citrus yella sooks your bloody cheeks in . . . the layoff in Essex was a godsend . . . a miracle . . . we're back on course with a vengeance! *(Springs to his feet)* You know what this is, don't you? It's a conspiracy, that's what it is! They don't *want* us to succeed . . .

COLQUHOUN: Who's 'they'?

MACBRYDE: *Them*, Robert . . . *them*! Out there . . . you've seen them, you've met them . . . *they . . . them . . .*

COLQUHOUN: The word's out on Bond Street . . . We stink, Bobby.

MACBRYDE: What you talkin' about 'we stink'? You're just after agreein' with me that we've never done better work!

COLQUHOUN: *Five* paintin's in . . . what is it . . . fourteen months?

MACBRYDE: We're talkin' *quality*, ya stupid bastard . . . it takes time to produce quality . . . an' sit up straight when I'm talkin' to you, stop actin' like they've got us strapped, they havenae! Look at me . . . they havenae . . . right!

COLQUHOUN: It isnae *they* . . . it isnae *them* . . . it's us . . . *you* an' *me*, Bobby . . . can you not see? 'Colquhoun and Macbryde' . . . *we're* the ones we've got to fight, not *them* . . . *us* . . . *us* . . . *fucking* us!

(*Silence.*)

MACBRYDE: Is it because we're Scottish, is that what it is?

COLQUHOUN: Aw, for God's sake . . .

(*Slumps back on to bed.*)

MACBRYDE: It's the kilts, isn't it? They hate us. They hate the fact that we've got a national dress an' a different language an' the Auld Alliance.

COLQUHOUN: The 'Auld' what?

MACBRYDE: . . . Alliance . . . Scotland an' France . . . they hate the Frogs even worse than they hate the fuckin' Jocks . . . dammit to hell, Rab, you've been rated above the likes of Nash an' Piper an' the rest of the so-called 'cream' of British Painting . . . Robert Melville, Herbert Read, Wyndham bloody Lewis, they've all said so . . . 'The most adroit and accomplished painter of the decade' . . . 'the most gifted draughtsman since Delacroix . . .'

COLQUHOUN: There you go again . . . overeggin' the puddin' . . . it wasnae 'Delacroix', it was 'Dadd', Richard Dadd, a minor Victorian 'genre' painter . . . Delacroix was a colossus, Dadd was a fuckin' daftie . . . all your energy goes into beatin' your bloody chest an' bayin' at the moon, small wonder you've got damn all left to put into your paintin'!

MACBRYDE: I've got what?

COLQUHOUN: You heard . . . you're just a bloody windbag! It doesnae surprise me there isnae a gallery that'll touch us! You're a blowhard an' a troublemaker, always were an' always will be, now, shuttup an' let me get some rest, I'm totally shattered!

(*He falls back on to bed, exhausted.* MACBRYDE *stands silent, face red, eyes bulging. Then his face breaks into a broad smile.*)

59

MACBRYDE: That's the stuff, Rab . . . Christ, for a minute there I
    thought the fire in your belly had snuffed it . . . c'mon, get
    your coat, we're steppin' out to fan the flames . . .
    (*Grabs Colquhoun's coat, hauls* COLQUHOUN *to his feet*.)
COLQUHOUN: What you doin'? I don't want to *step* out . . .
MACBRYDE: Aye, you bloody do . . . we'll tap a coupla quid an'
    get absolutely steamboats . . .
COLQUHOUN: . . . aaachoo!
MACBRYDE: . . . Skinful of booze will do you the world of good,
    Robert, buck you up no end.
    (*Exeunt*.)
COLQUHOUN: (*Off*) Aaaaaaaaachoo!

Lights fade to half. Two BAILIFFS *enter. They start carrying furniture
out into street where they dump it in a big pile.*
A light snow starts to fall. Exeunt BAILIFFS.
Enter ADLER *pushing a handcart. He parks the handcart and climbs
up on to pile of furniture and broken canvases. Sits and waits.*
Pause.
We hear COLQUHOUN *and* MACBRYDE *approach before we see them.*
MACBRYDE: (*Off. Sings*)
        The snow is snowing, the cold wind blowing . . .
        but we can weather the storm . . .
COLQUHOUN: (*Off*) Aaaaaachoo!
    (*They stagger into view, arm in arm, drunk*.)
COLQUHOUN/MACBRYDE: (*Together*)
        . . . Who cares how much it may storm,
        we've got our love to keep us warm . . .
COLQUHOUN: . . . aachoo!
MACBRYDE: Aw, look, Robert . . .
    (*They peer at* ADLER *in the gloom sitting on top of the pile of
    debris*.)
COLQUHOUN: . . . a pixie.
MACBRYDE: . . . more like a fuckin' elf. (*Loudly*) Ho, you the
    mischievous fucker that used to stitch ma eyelids thegither
    durin' the night?
ADLER: Five hours I been sitting here keeping an eye out for zis
    pile of junk, vere ze hell you been?

(COLQUHOUN *pokes drunkenly around pile of furniture.*)

COLQUHOUN: Nice bed, Jankel . . . me an' Robert's got one not entirely dissimilar . . .

(ADLER *clambers down off his perch.*)

ADLER: I brungk youse a barra.

COLQUHOUN: What's happenin', you flittin'? Adler's flittin', Robert . . .

(MACBRYDE *circles pile of furniture.*)

ADLER: I'd offer to put youse up on ze flooring but I am crushed into a vee corner of a second-storey basement in Battersea . . .

MACBRYDE: Small wonder we couldnae find you . . . we had to get a lend of some dough from . . . hold on, what's ma paintbox doin' out here?

COLQUHOUN: *And* your easel . . . or is it mine?

ADLER: As soon you get anuzzer place to live, let me know, I come collect ze barra . . .

(*Turns to go.*)

MACBRYDE: Adler!

ADLER: Vot . . . you zink ze peoples zat own zese buildingks are daft zey rent to artists ven zey can zell to city gents vit zere whores zey vant stick avay in a hideyhole apartment zo zere vives don't find out? You are children, ze pair of you . . . vatch out for zat barra, ze veeels are shoogly.

(*Exits.*)

MACBRYDE: I don't know about you, Rab, but I didnae understand a bloody word of that . . .

COLQUHOUN: Hey, Bobby . . . this is *our* bed.

(*Starts sifting through furniture.*)

MACBRYDE: Aye, an' I wouldnae mind gettin' into it, I'm shagged out . . .

(*Staggers towards front door. Loudly*) . . . Open up, ya bastards!

COLQUHOUN: . . . *and* the rugs, *and* the chairs.

MACBRYDE: Awright, if that's how you want it. Stand back, Rab . . . stand back, everybody . . .

(*Backs off in order to take a run at front door and break it down . . . trips, falls backwards.*)

. . . ahyah, bugger!

(*Crunching sound of breaking glass.* COLQUHOUN'*s head snaps round.*)

Oh oh . . .

(*Reaches into pocket, withdraws broken-off neck of whisky bottle.*)

. . . sorry.

COLQUHOUN: (*Stunned*) I don't believe it.

MACBRYDE: I said I was sorry . . .

(*Clambers to his feet.*)

COLQUHOUN: I don't fuckin' believe it, you've broke it, ya clown!

MACBRYDE: Aye, awright, awright, I fell backwards on to ma arse an' broke the whisky bottle on purpose just to annoy you if that makes you any happier, now shuttup moanin' an let's get this pile of junk on to that . . .

COLQUHOUN: (*Overlapping*) You hate me, ya clumsy shite, that's why you broke it . . . you've always hated me . . . on you go, say it . . . say it . . . you hate me . . . say it!

MACBRYDE: Awright, anythin' for a bit of peace an' quiet . . . I hate you, how's that? Ever since I clapped eyes on you at the Art School I've hated you . . .

(*Starts piling furniture on to handcart.* COLQUHOUN *joins in.*)

COLQUHOUN: I knew it . . . I knew it!

MACBRYDE: . . . you're a whiner, a sniveller, a liar and a self-pityin' bastard!

COLQUHOUN: Ma Uncle Jamesie was right . . .

MACBRYDE: Not only are you sarcastic, stingy, and xenophobic, you're physically repulsive into the bargain . . .

COLQUHOUN: . . . you're an unattractive wee cunt!

MACBRYDE: . . . as for your personal habits, the least offensive of which are bed-wettin', wipin' your arse on the sheets, not washin' your oxters, an' blowin' your nose on ma kilt when I'm not lookin', the less said the better!

COLQUHOUN: You repel and revolt me . . . your very presence in a room is enough to make my stomach heave, my bowels loosen, my very viscera to shrink and shrivel . . . all of which I'm telling you, not because it makes me feel better but in the certain knowledge that it will cause you pain!

MACBRYDE: You know what you are, don't you? You're a fuckin'
sadist . . . only a fuckin' sadist would force me to blurt out all
these home truths whilst manhandlin' a pile of dud furniture
on to a wonky barra bound for Christ only knows where
without a bloody dram!
(*They have ended up with just as much furniture on the ground as
before.* COLQUHOUN *stares down at broken canvas.* MACBRYDE
starts reloading stuff on to handcart. Stops.)
Well, don't just stand there, give us a bloody . . .
(COLQUHOUN *falls to his knees, clutches broken canvas and
starts to cry.* MACBRYDE *comes across several more broken
canvases amongst the debris.*)
. . . aw, no.
(*Stares at vandalized canvases in disbelief.*)
COLQUHOUN: (*Fiercely, to himself*) Why, why, why, why??
(MACBRYDE *crosses, touches* COLQUHOUN's *shoulder.*)
MACBRYDE: C'mon, sweetheart, it's not the end of the world . . .
(COLQUHOUN *sobs.* MACBRYDE *helps him to his feet. They hold
on to one another.* MACBRYDE *too starts to cry. They cross slowly
to handcart, pick up broken canvases, load them tenderly on to
pile of debris. Lights slowly down. Pause.*)
(*In blackout*) Y'there, Robert?
COLQUHOUN: No.
MACBRYDE: I've been thinkin' . . .
COLQUHOUN: Well, don't.
MACBRYDE: (*Strikes match*) . . . see, ever since I was wee?
(*Public toilet flushes very nearby.*)
I've always wanted to live in a cottage.
COLQUHOUN: Yes, very droll. Goodnight. (*Blows match out.
Pause.*)
MACBRYDE: (*In blackout. Sings*)
     Ae fond kiss and then we sever . . .
     Ae fareweel and so for ever . . .
COLQUHOUN: Shuttup!

Lights slowly up on Cork Street. COLQUHOUN *with his back to us
looking very scruffy. Enter* MACBRYDE, *also scruffy, with large
battered portfolio.*

MACBRYDE: Supercilious wee shitebag! 'Course he knew who we were, we used to drink in the fuckin' Colony with the bastard . . . I remember lendin' him a tenner. Poncin' about in a fuckin' three-piece suit like he *owns* that fuckin' gallery . . .

COLQUHOUN: I think he does.

MACBRYDE: . . . where else would he get monotypes at a fiver a throw? They're all *signed*, for Christ's sake! It's not all that long ago people were fightin' one another to get their filthy mitts on a Robert Colquhoun original . . . c'mon, we'll nip round to Arthur Tooth's, see if *they'll* bite . . .
(*Sets off. Stops.*) . . . you listenin', Rab, I said . . . what you starin' at?

COLQUHOUN: The Future, Bobby.

MACBRYDE: Eh?
(*Lights up on enormous Jackson Pollock canvas.*)
Sufferin' Christ, what's that??

COLQUHOUN: About fifty cents' worth of stove enamel dribbled on to a big sheet of hardboard an' framed up nice.
(MACBRYDE *stares at painting, slack-jawed.*)

MACBRYDE: Ach, another six months an' they'll not be able to *give* this stuff away.

COLQUHOUN: They're givin' this one away right now for seven and a half thousand . . .

MACBRYDE: Seven an' a half grand for a chunk of wallpaper? They must be jokin'!

COLQUHOUN: Aye, an' guess who the laugh's on?

MACBRYDE: It's a passin' fad, Robert . . . a circus turn . . . a variety . . . show. Fuck.

COLQUHOUN: The hacks are already dolin' out black armbands in Bond Street an' laughin' all the way to their newspaper offices . . . 'Europe Is Dead . . . God Bless America!' C'mon, I'll race you to the Colony, bound to be some old piss artist we can cadge a coupla drinks off . . . c'mon, I said! (*Drags* MACBRYDE *away.*)

MACBRYDE: (*Over shoulder, to Jackson Pollock*) Fuckin' wallpaper!
(*Exeunt. Lights slowly down.*)

Lights up on scummy bedsit in Islington. A filthy mattress on the floor.
COLQUHOUN *huddled over drawing board. A bare light bulb. Loud rumble of Underground train. Room shakes.*

COLQUHOUN: 'Small, self-contained "studio" flat, comfortably
    appointed . . . handy for Tube . . . suit two gentlemen . . .
    non-smokers preferred . . .' (*Glancing up*) . . . the back end
    of Fifty-Seven . . . Oliver Hardy, the corpulent half of the
    famous comedy twosome, dies at the age of sixty five . . . the
    long-awaited Wolfenden Report recommends that
    homosexual acts between consenting adult men in private
    should no longer constitute a crime, and the Russians, much
    to the vexation of the Yanks, are ahead in the Space Race
    with the launch of Sputnik One . . . (*Glancing up at ceiling*)
    . . . aw, aye, an' Jackson Pollock's 'Blue Poles' is sold at
    auction for one million, three hundred thousand dollars . . . a
    clear case of the 'Future' overtaking the present.
    (*Lights up on* MACBRYDE, *dirty and unkempt, pacing to and fro,*
    tumbler in fist, in his stocking feet.)
    Bobby and I are still hard at it, of course . . . we've got an
    exhibition comin' up in Huddersfield an' a breach of the
    peace charge in November . . . things are fairly hectic at the
    minute what with this new ballet at Covent Garden, but once
    that's over we can crack on with . . .
MACBRYDE: (*Overlapping*) 'Decor' . . . aye, that's it . . . 'Decor'
    . . . 'Costumes and Decor . . . Colquhoun and Macbryde' . . .
    d'you think we should ask for it up in lights . . . or not?
COLQUHOUN: (*Returning to drawings*) Remember an' give me
    them socks off, they're stinkin' the place out.
MACBRYDE: 'Colquhoun an' Macbryde, Costumes an' Decor' . . .
    forty watt bulbs, assorted colours . . . compound the felony,
    Robert . . .
    (COLQUHOUN *carries on working.*)
    . . . compound the felony, Rab . . . we're already a laughing
    stock so why not go the whole hog an' *compound the felony*
    . . . supply the bastards with the ammunition . . . no?
COLQUHOUN: It's work, Bobby.
MACBRYDE: 'Work'? Did you say 'work'? I remember the days
    when we never done any *work* . . . it just flowed . . . joyously,

effortlessly . . . we never had to think about it. Certainly not as *'work'*, Robert. Christ, when you think back to what we used to be . . . we used to be 'the Two Roberts', Rab . . . we used to be *Colquhoun an' MacBryde*, for fuck's sake!

COLQUHOUN: Don't.

MACBRYDE: Reporters used to ring us up an' ask us who we tipped to win the Gold Cup at Ascot . . . they used to snap us gettin' wur hair cut . . . we were invited everywhere . . . we were a *legend*, Robbie . . .

COLQUHOUN: Stop it.

MACBRYDE: . . . a fuckin' *legend*. No, I beg your pardon . . . *two* fuckin' legends . . . 'Coonmacbryde' . . . 'a single organism . . . strivin' towards', Rab? Eh? What was it this *'single organism'* was 'strivin' towards', Robert?

COLQUHOUN: I think you should go to your bed. (*He carries on working at costume drawings.*)

MACBRYDE: You.'re not goin' to tell me, are you?

(COLQUHOUN *ignores him.*)

Are you?

(COLQUHOUN *carries on working.*)

Awright, *don't* tell me . . . don't *you* tell *me*!

(*Pause.*)

Hold on, hold on . . . 'strivin' towards a . . . coherent somethin'', am I right? Am I right, Colquhoun? '. . . a coherent fuckin' something'-or-other', I'm fuckin' right, ya bastard!

(*He staggers against* COLQUHOUN, *spilling paint over costume drawings.* COLQUHOUN *springs to his feet.*)

COLQUHOUN: Now, look what you've done!

MACBRYDE: I'm sorry, Rab . . . here, let me . . .

(COLQUHOUN *hits him hard across the face, sending him to the floor.* MACBRYDE *looks bewildered, then starts to cry.*)

COLQUHOUN: Stop that.

MACBRYDE: I'm sorry, Rab . . .

COLQUHOUN: Stop it, I said.

MACBRYDE: I'm really, really sorry . . .

(*He crawls across and clings to* COLQUHOUN's *legs.*)

COLQUHOUN: Get away from me . . . get away! (*Tries to free*

66

himself. Can't.) . . . Get away, ya cunt!
(*He starts hitting* MACBRYDE. MACBRYDE *in tears.*)
MACBRYDE: Please, Robert . . . help me . . .
COLQUHOUN: (*Freeing himself*) Away to fuck.
MACBRYDE: (*Clambering to his feet*) Help me, Rab . . . (*He
staggers the few steps towards* COLQUHOUN, *falls to his knees
and looks up at him, his body wracked with sobs.*) . . . please.
(COLQUHOUN, *face set, immovable, staring into the distance.
Lights slowly down. Bring up* MACBRYDE *singing 'Ae Fond
Kiss'. Curtain.*)